RONAROSE TRAIN

ANNY & ME
From TEXAS to TAIWAN

White Station
PUBLISHING, LLC

A White Station Publishing, LLC Production
ANNY & ME
from Texas to Taiwan

Text © 2021 by RONAROSE TRAIN

Copyright © 2021

All rights reserved. No part of this book may be reproduced in any form, by any electronic or mechanical means, including information storage and retrieval systems, without permission in writing from the publisher, except by a reviewer who may quote brief passages in a review.

Requests for permission to make copies of any part of this work should be sent to address below:

White Station Publishing, LLC
www.whitestationpublishing.com
First Edition
Book layout and cover design by Ira S. Van Scoyoc
Illustration by Willow Van Scoyoc Taylour

Printed in the United States of America

DEDICATION

I dedicate ANNY AND ME to ...

Anny, for our special friendship which transcends cultures and distance.

The entire Shen family, for their love, warmth, and extraordinary hospitality.

Punkin Hecht, for encouraging me to publish the story.

Carol and Michael Wilk, for being a part of the story.

And always L.A., for his love and support.

INTRODUCTION

"You must see the origami exhibit," Anny Shen said to the group who had just joined us. "Winston and Alice will escort you." She turned to me. "You and I will visit the armor collection."

It was a cold day in March of 2017. We were two women, a Taiwanese and an American, old friends whose similarities transcended our ten-year difference in age and diverse cultures. Accompanied by her son Winston and his beautiful wife Alice, we had spent several hours admiring an extensive display at Tainan's Chimei Museum. At last Anny and I could enjoy each other, alone.

I nodded, knowing her intention. We sought more time together, as my visit to Taiwan was growing short. Arms entwined, our shoulders touching, we walked through the exhibit which didn't interest either of us.

As always, I noticed heads turned to observe this foreigner in locations where few Americans were seen. Anny had taken me to many such places. Our friendship gave me a window into another world, with thoughtful adjustments to make it easier for me. In consideration of most Westerners' lack of Chinese fluency, for example, our friends adopted English names which we could easily pronounce. I found Anny's world to be comparable in many ways to my own. We each had raised our children, cared for our elders, grown older with our husbands, and faced crises of health and politics. We lived parallel lives, separated only by geography.

"Not so much to see," Anny said as we stood in the entry and studied the entire armor display from there.

"Let's walk around the room," I said. "We can read the information on the signs. It's so nice that we're here together."

"Yes."

It was a peaceful and warm feeling to share the time with Anny. We were able to communicate, but chatting about any and everything as I did with other friends wasn't possible, simply because neither of us was skilled enough in the other's language. Despite this shortcoming, I felt a closeness that went beyond words. Only later did I reflect on the intimacy we shared when it was only the two of us without translators present. Though I didn't know all I could have known about my friend Anny, for me our strong and enduring connection did not require anything more than being in her presence.

We leisurely browsed our way around the few presentations, until we spied the museum shop. "That looks like our next stop," I said, and we didn't need to discuss it.

Browsing among the gifts and souvenirs, we simultaneously noticed the stack of coloring books for adults.

"I want to buy one for you," Anny said, speaking slowly and distinctly. Smiling, she reached for a packet with a creative cover design, the one I had already spotted.

As usual, our thoughts were alike. "No, I want to give one to you," I said, slowly and distinctly. Because Anny seemed to first think in Chinese and then speak in English, I had learned to allow her time to translate in her mind.

"You are my guest," she insisted, surely believing her point trumped mine.

The solution was obvious. We each purchased a set and with broad smiles and ceremonial bows, presented them to each other. That moment summarized our unique bond. We were friends from seemingly opposite worlds whose values and principles were similar.

I had met the wife of our business associate in 1994 on my first trip to Taiwan. An exquisite young woman in her thirties dressed in the latest designer clothes, she immediately captured my heart. Sometimes you just know a dear friend from the first moment, and our connection was instantaneous. Though in the intervening years our times together were few, we cherished our unique relationship. We were soul sisters.

THE BEGINNING

One fall afternoon in 1981, Julie Shen ventured into a branch of our family business -- Swiff-Train Company's San Antonio office. She was in her twenties, fit and energetic, and determined.

Taiwanese, she was recently divorced and looking for something to do. She had convinced her father she wanted to remain in Houston and could cover her expenses by selling Winton Tile, the vinyl flooring product her family manufactured in Taiwan.

Kenny, the eldest Train brother, knew the product he was holding was not right for his Texas market.

Julie sighed. "Truthfully, Mr. Train, I've seen other distributors in the United States. Those in Texas told me to see your family because you understand how to import."

My brother-in-law Kenny examined the tile. "These patterns and colors aren't popular in Texas." He smiled at Julie and said, "But maybe we can work something out." He sent her to see his father and brother in Corpus Christi.

Herbert Train and his middle son, L.A., recognized an opportunity, and proposed, "If you ship all of it to our warehouse at your expense, we won't charge for storage, and we'll pay you as we sell it."

They found customers who wanted an economical, easy way to cover their floor, and in time sold all of Julie's inventory. Sales grew by creating new patterns, adapting designs from their most popular sheet vinyl. The company was truly ahead of its time, and with Winton Tile they were in the forefront of a new product that the United States flooring industry and the public didn't know nor understand. Their challenge was to educate them.

Swiff-Train introduced untraditional flooring customers to new possibilities. Apartment maintenance personnel could quickly replace a bathroom floor, eliminating the need for and expense of professionals. The do-it-yourselfer didn't have to know much to give his wife's kitchen a new look.

It was August 1987 when my husband L.A. invited me to leave my career as a Realtor in that disastrous financial recession of the 1980s and join Swiff-Train Company. I was 45 years old, our three children were in college, and though I had been married to our family business for 25 years, I knew nothing about our products. But I learned, and peddled flooring of all types, including Winton Tile. Their product energized our business as we struggled to recover from the recession.

Herbert Train retired in 1986, and his three sons ran the day-to-day business. Kenny and L.A. focused on Sales, while the youngest brother Jeffrey managed Operations. By then, I had transitioned from a sales territory into the Purchasing Department, and when a consultant introduced me to Total Quality Management, the Train brothers appointed me to lead the initiative. This concept of utilizing teams to improve processes and procedures proved to be the answer to streamlining our business and managing growth.

As sales increased, Swiff-Train added staff and opened more branches throughout Texas. The early 1990s saw L.A. and Kenny travel to Europe, Mexico, and South America to exhibit Winton Tile in trade shows, adding customers and further expanding the business. We Trains met with Julie Shen frequently, and she became a friend as well as a supplier. L.A. spent many a late evening on the phone with her as she translated across different time zones between him and her brother Jyi-fong in Taiwan.

In the spring of 1994, the Winton Tile sales had grown so much that a trip to the factory was necessary. I was thrilled to accompany my husband and his brother Kenny for the first of many visits.

TAINAN MAY 1994

L.A. and I flew from Texas to Taipei, the capital of Taiwan. I can still feel the butterflies arcing circles in my stomach as I anticipated the long flight and the opportunity to experience a vastly different culture.

I had met Jyi-fong Shen at the yearly Las Vegas trade shows. Clearly he was the boss. He governed the business negotiations in Taiwanese, translated by his sister Julie. Though his limited English fluency kept him from conversing socially, his warm manner and many toasts made us feel important. I was not traveling to strangers, but to see friends and to meet the rest of their family.

L.A. and I naturally enjoyed people, and the thought of getting to know the Shen family was exhilarating and exciting. It was a rare opportunity. Anticipating a unique and memorable experience, I began a journal to capture every tidbit I could savor for years to come. Little did I know that for me the trip would be life-changing.

"We have made all the flight arrangements for you," Julie told us. "It will be fourteen hours, so I'm sending you a book to study. You can be fluent in Chinese by the time you land in Taipei." Was she serious? I did learn a few phrases with the help of Julie's book, and the nice young man in the next seat aided my pronunciation. We ate authentic Taiwanese food on the EVA airlines flight, different from the Texas version of Asian. Our seats were next to the bathrooms and the traffic all night was constant and noisy, but we collected several of those tiny airline pillows and slept fitfully. Crossing the International Date Line put our arrival at Taipei's Chiang Kai Shek airport to be the next morning plus a day later. We were fated to begin our Taiwan experience in a state of exhaustion.

I saw Julie running to meet us, with a beautiful woman close behind. She was Jyi-fong's wife Anny. We hugged both women and an equally tired Kenny, who had arrived earlier because the Train boys never flew together. We knew of a family who were not so foresighted, and we learned from their tragedy. It was a relief to see Julie, to know that we were in the hands of a native who knew her way around and was our friend.

"I'm so glad to see you! Are you too tired? How was the flight?" Julie seemed as pleased to see us as we were to see her. I hoped she was prepared to spend the next several days facilitating discussions and negotiations between our two families -- and doing it in two languages.

"Anny, I am so glad to finally meet you," I said slowly and distinctly. "Julie has told me such nice things about you."

"I am happy to meet you, too," Anny replied, slowly and distinctly. She had been studying English, and I admired her effort to tackle sounds and writing completely different from her own. I was embarrassed that I had no knowledge of her language.

My first impression remained the same throughout our years together. I immediately was smitten. No translation was necessary for me to glean that Anny was a beautiful, intelligent, refined woman with an occasional impish grin revealing a cute sense of humor. I have always wished I had her natural grace and elegance.

Anny linked her arm in mine and, touching shoulders as we walked, guided me to claim our luggage and then to the waiting driver and van. I felt honored by her attention. To me it was a welcome and comforting gesture. I knew I had made a new friend.

Julie informed us that Anny had reserved the finest hotel in Tainan, but for the night we would stay in Taipei at the airport's Chiang Kai Shek Hotel, run by the Taiwanese government. The personnel were polite, despite being overwhelmed with so much to do and so few co-workers.

Entering our nondescript, plain room, L.A. and I dropped to the very low bed, exhausted. "Wow, this is as hard as a board," I said. "How will we ever be able to sleep?" We found that all our beds in Taiwan were just like that first one: exceptionally hard and surprisingly comfortable. We had no more backaches or sciatica. Within a year we purchased a Taiwanese mattress for ourselves and shipped it to Texas.

Our first Asian breakfast buffet presented L.A., Kenny, and me an overwhelming array. There were dumplings with various fillings, and a loose unflavored rice gruel called congee, with condiments to add as you please: preserved ginger, chopped peanuts, shredded foodstuff we couldn't identify, and dried fish. We sampled oriental cakes and enjoyed delicious fresh tangerine juice. And there were fried rice, noodles, meats, and some items the nature of which we had no clue. Our morning cup of coffee was so strong it was really black, with no cream to be found. The only familiar breakfast foods were eggs and some cereals.

The Shens' van driver, Mr. Wu, transported the five of us two hours south from Taipei to Taichung. "How interesting that all the major cities begin with 'Tai,'" I remarked to Julie.

"It's simple," she taught us. "'Tai' refers to Taiwan. 'pei' signifies north, 'chung' means middle, and 'nan' is south." I got it. Taipei, Taichung, and Tainan indicated their geographic location on the island of Taiwan. We were going to visit them all.

Mr. Yu, owner of a printing factory, and his manager, also Mr. Yu, were our hosts in their city of Taichung. We checked into the first-class Evergreen Hotel, with marble and polished woods and classic elegance. We had left government accommodations for the finer side.

Jyi-fong met us at the hotel. Lunch began an adventure featuring authentic Taiwanese food, and not a fork in sight. They politely ignored my chopstick incompetence as I chased the food around my plate until I captured some. It was a great way to lose a few pounds.

I came to appreciate Chinese culture. It was considered impolite and uncomfortable to acknowledge another's difficulty in doing something, such as my chopstick challenge. According to custom, they didn't look, didn't comment, didn't laugh. They kindly gave their guests a bit of time to try, and if it still didn't turn out well, they could then politely step in and offer to correct. When I laughed at myself, that released the Shens to stop pretending and give me instruction. I was a slow learner. A difference in culture could cause misunderstanding or chasm in friendship, but not in ours. The Shens were so gracious and good-natured that I never felt embarrassed or stressed. And they always were considerate enough to order a fork for me.

Dining with Anny was a ritual, another example of our different cultures. She was in charge of me. I felt that she valued and wanted to honor me with special attention, and I was happy to be in her care. From our first meal together, our connection was physical as well as spiritual, to the extent that we sat so close together that we were almost on the same chair. Our shoulders often touched as Anny reached to serve the delicious dishes she had ordered. It was a warm and comforting feeling to be so in sync, and even though we had just met, I recognized our compatibility.

Using her chopsticks, Anny kept my plate full of delicacies and encouraged me to eat, assuring me it was good. And every dish was exceptionally good. Our hosts were considerate and often told us what we were consuming, and we three foreigners were brave enough to try most of it. Chewy marinated tiny fish. Seaweed salad. Steaming soup with bits of fish and tiny pork meatballs. We quickly noticed that the Shens habitually ordered an exorbitant number of courses, and learned it was another cultural practice that began in ancient times. Emperors exhibited their respect of their guests by the magnitude of the banquet. No matter the guest's status, it was important to be polite and honorable hosts. We guests happily expressed our appreciation of their hospitality by sampling it all, until we must proclaim that we cannot eat another bite. It always takes several declarations before they accept.

Chinese culture dictates a show of respect in every possible circumstance. Thus, in gatherings large or small, toasts show regard and make guests feel honored, welcomed and accepted. Jyi-fong honored each of us -- repeatedly. Scotch, wine, beer – it didn't matter. We returned the sentiments. Sated with food and euphoric with too many toasts, the Shens and Trains nevertheless proceeded to combine business with pleasure. I quickly concluded that Chinese culture was going to keep me overweight and inebriated. I could have gotten used to that.

Anny spent the rest of the day on her own, and I joined the men and Julie. I observed the sights as Mr. Wu drove us to Mr. and Mr. Yu's factory. At that time, Taiwan was densely populated with twenty-six million people on the small island. Cars, buses, and trucks of all kinds, plus moped scooters by the thousands flooded the streets. All imported vehicles paid duty equal to 100% of the purchase price, and 99% of the vehicles we saw were imported. No wonder there were so many mopeds; they were cheap compared to cars and trucks. Few cyclists wore helmets, but many wore face masks to protect from the air pollution of so many vehicles and so much manufacturing in their country. As there was no zoning, a factory could be next to a condominium building. In the non-industrial areas, all buildings were multi-story, generally with commercial enterprises on the first few floors and dwellings above. People didn't rent apartments, they purchased condominiums according to their means. Julie informed us that it was still the custom, caused by economic as well as traditional reasons, for several generations of a family to occupy one residence.

Following our afternoon at the printing factory, we rested at the hotel until Mr. Wu arrived to drive us to dinner at a huge three-story seafood restaurant. It was packed almost to capacity, and as far as I could see, we were the only Western diners. The Misters Yu, Julie, Jyi-fong, and Anny escorted us to the display of fresh seafood on ice as well as live fish and shellfish in tanks. "Now you must select your dinner," Julie informed us. I chose a lobster and silently apologized to the crustacean for its sacrifice.

Our friendship progressed, thanks to Julie's willingness to translate to supplement Anny's English. Conversations were slow but we allowed each other time to think, and we began to explore each other's way of life.

"How many children?" Each of us had three.

"What do you like to do?" We both enjoyed cooking. Took care of our families. Worked in our family businesses. It was exciting to know we had so much in common.

I enjoyed Anny's attention as we leaned comfortably against each other while she continually filled my plate. I savored the parade of beautifully prepared and presented dishes and drank coconut milk, beer, and scotch. Though I never liked scotch, after several beers, it didn't matter to me what I imbibed for Jyi-fong's nonstop toasts.

Soon it was time for the inevitable. "Julie, not knowing your language, I can't ask anyone else. Could you please show me the way to the bathroom?"

She did but didn't show me how to use it.

I opened the door to the stall and saw there was one step up, with a urinal-looking fixture embedded in the marble floor. Like a puppy, I walked around the thing a few times, considering how I could get my appropriate anatomy down there. Despite my high heels and panty hose, I finally did it. Restricted by lowered panty hose binding my thighs, unbalanced on my high heels, and fearful of falling into the apparatus in the floor, I needed help to stand. Something to hold on to. My only possibility was the door handle, and it was behind me. I had faced the wrong direction. It was then that I remembered photos of Asians eating, working, playing games in a squat position. Now I understood the design of the stall and cursed myself for neglecting exercise to develop stronger quads. There was no possibility of turning around, so I considered my options. When young, my brothers could shimmy up a door frame by applying force from their hands and feet. It's physics. I could do it, too. There was no other choice. I mustered all the force I could and walked my hands up the walls, pushing the floor with my feet and leaning forward to avoid falling back into the bowl. I did it! I was standing! Thankful, I vowed to begin an exercise regimen as soon as I returned home. For sure. Probably.

Julie appeared just as I exited the bathroom. "Are you alright? You were away so long that I was worried about you." When I explained my situation, she laughed.

"Oh, Rona, I am so sorry. I should have realized you've never seen this style," and with my permission, she ran to tell the men about her inexperienced visitor. When I returned to the group, all were merrily laughing and applauding. I joined in the fun and expected to be the subject of more laughter when they repeated my story the next day.

It was late, and all but Jyi-fong declined the Yus' invitation to go nightclubbing. The rest of us returned to the hotel and Julie treated us to massages in our rooms. In Taiwan, we learned, the best masseurs are blind so that they are not distracted. They massage by pushing on pressure points to release your tension, but my little blind masseuse was too industrious. She found the spots that hurt the most, the ones with the poorest circulation. It was not hard to find them again. The next morning, I nursed deep purple bruises and a killer headache.

After breakfast, our contingent met the Misters Yu for a tour through their new printing factory. Though Anny considerately offered to sit with me in the comfortably air conditioned office instead of touring the factory, I declined. Like my siblings, I inherited our father's interest in how things are made. I always loved factories, and enjoyed learning about the newer equipment, larger facility, and more efficiently designed layout that would improve their process. Manager Yu described the functions and specifics of each piece of equipment and Julie translated his explanation. I was confused until we moved to the next space and realized that I had misunderstood which machine he meant. I pointed to the large apparatus we were approaching and said to Kenny, " That's the machine he told us about in the last room."

I was smug, elated that I knew what I was looking at.

Though I didn't think Kenny was impressed, my Daddy would have been proud.

Owner Yu insisted we follow him to make one stop before driving to Tainan. We waited in the van, Anny and me sitting together as usual, while he ran into a shop and returned with a package. Smiling broadly, he presented the gift to me: a beautifully wrapped assortment of Taiwanese cakes. I was flattered, and repeated xie-xie several times to thank him. Julie explained that those cakes were famous in Taichung, and he had chosen the special present to show his appreciation of our family's visit. It was a great honor to receive such a tribute, and again I thanked him in behalf of our family and our company.

While Mr. Wu drove us to Tainan on a modern highway, we five spent part of the two hours' time gratefully napping. Anny's head occasionally drifted on to my shoulder and probably I did the same. When I wasn't dozing, I found the countryside interesting. The vista was a mixture of narrow winding roads with low houses and small cafes, clusters of several-story buildings that looked to me like houses, and farmland. No fences, no sidewalks. People wearing pointed straw hats tended cows and goats. Traveling at high speed in the latest model air conditioned van, I was struck by the juxtaposition of the ancient and the modern. I tried to remember details of the fascinating ride to include in my journal.

My first impression of the Shens' city was of an interrupted economy. We passed hundreds of high-rise buildings under construction, partially completed, surrounded by scaffolding, with few workers in sight. The population density seemed similar to that of Taipei and Taichung, with thousands of people riding thousands of mopeds. It was amazing to see several passengers on one moped or bulky loads of various descriptions piled together on these small vehicles. I marveled at the brave drivers as they made their way among the weaving cars and trucks. There were no lanes, just a system of every man for himself. If there was a tiny space, some vehicle quickly filled it. Mr. Wu smoothly maneuvered us through the melee and deposited us Texans for a quick check-in at the New Tainan Hotel. There was no time allowed to rest before our next stop, the Shens' Winton Tile factory.

It was nestled on a narrow winding street among other similar businesses. The metal structures sat at all angles, as if a tornado had whirled them off the ground and mischievously redeposited them. My first sight upon entering the complex was an old man, bare chested and sweating as he shoveled vinyl scraps into a yawning container emitting high heat. I learned that it was a Banbury mixer, invented in 1916 to increase efficiency of rubber tire production needed to supply the growing demand for automobiles. The Winton Tile process combined new, or virgin, vinyl with trimmings from their production, using the machine to apply heat and pressure as it pulverized and mixed the vinyl. I thought of the blazing fires of hell and saw that this lone man was intent on doing a good job in the extreme heat, not at all weary or slow. The production workers also seemed to be confident in their jobs and smiled or nodded to us in greeting as we toured. They looked sharp in their shirts sporting the Winton Tile logo. We said hello to everyone with one of our newly learned words: *ni' hao*, accompanying the greeting with our own smiles and nods.

After our short visit, the men and Julie rode with Jyi-fong in his car, and I followed Anny to hers. I knew we were going to visit their home, and though I had no idea what to expect, I was excited to be allowed a glimpse of their family environment. Conversation was minimal as Anny navigated traffic. She occasionally asked me questions, slowly and distinctly, and I had the feeling that she had carefully constructed the English before speaking. I would have done the same if I had been ambitious enough to study Chinese. I answered slowly and waited for her to repeat my answer to me, confirming that she understood. How old are your children? What do you like to cook?

We drove through busy streets, and most of the buildings seemed to have shops and restaurants on the first floor and apartments or offices occupying several stories above. She slowed on a street just like the others, and I expected her to park parallel to the sidewalk like the few cars I had seen. Instead, Anny expertly executed a maneuver to angle perpendicular, facing a store front covered by a metal door. I didn't understand why we were positioned in front of a shop that was obviously closed, until Anny removed a remote control from her purse and touched a button. It was in fact a garage door, rising on a track like ours at home, and she drove her Mercedes on to the marble floor. Thinking of our own concrete-floored garage, I was impressed and couldn't wait to see the interior of their home.

We entered through a door in the far wall, and my men were already there, waiting for us. They beat us by several minutes. I noticed L.A.'s somber expression and asked him what was on his mind. He whispered, "Kenny and I thought we were passengers in a Nascar race. Jyi-fong is fearless."

"I'm glad I rode with Anny," I laughed as our host began the tour.

The house was much larger than the street frontage indicated. We were in a long, narrow, marble-floored room with several staircases leading to a second story mezzanine and walled private areas on either side. Julie and Jyi-fong grew up there. Their parents' rooms were up the far staircase, and now Anny's young family occupied the near upstairs rooms.

Past the staircases the space widened to seating areas furnished in carved and comfortable Chinese classic style mixed with contemporary. On the first floor were guest bedrooms and a large kitchen with modern appliances. I wondered how the Shen women shared that space. Was there a master and a sous chef, a general and a soldier, or two companions working in harmony to feed their loved ones? Even with my limited knowledge of the Shen family, I bet on the latter.

Boldly striped orange and white Koi glided in a sunken marble fish pond nestled under the closest stairs.

Julie told us that their culture attributes many positive qualities to the koi such as courage, overcoming adversity, the ability to attain the highest goals, and strong character. Their presence guaranteed good luck. I'd vote for that.

Speaking Chinese and using gestures which needed no translation, the elder Mr. Shen welcomed us to his home. He was a trim and energetic man whom I judged to be in his late sixties and had recently retired to travel the world. He pointed to the gallery overlooking the fish pond, and Julie explained that her father wanted us to see his ivory collection. We climbed the elegant near staircase with its elaborate wrought iron railing and entered the glass-sided room to admire his museum-quality display of scrimshaw and antique tusks. Mrs. Shen waited to greet us as we descended the stairs, broadly smiling and taking my hand to convey hospitality in a universal language.

Anny introduced us to her daughters, pretty girls who were about 14 and 12 and had little interest in such strange-looking guests. I didn't see their 10-year-old, until he zoomed into the room on roller skates. L.A., Kenny, and I were speechless to see the boy racing around the marble floor inside the house, but Jyi-fong laughed in delight. I suspected he would have liked to join his son.

When the business discussions began, Anny invited me to accompany her to drive Mrs. Shen to see a friend. Though Julie had described the arrangement as very congenial, I wondered how Anny felt about living in her mother-in-law's home. When we were alone after taking Mrs. Shen to her friend, I boldly asked her what it was like.

Anny seemed to process the question. She turned to me and matter-of-factly answered. "It is our custom." It was as simple as that.

It had been a long day, but the agenda included just a short time for us to rest and freshen up. As much as I longed to burrow under the covers of the tempting bed and remain for the night, I set an alarm to allow at least a quick nap.

We were ready on time with smiles and renewed energy. We needed it for the full evening the Shens had planned. Dinner was Japanese cuisine, with a talented chef stationed behind a griddle putting on a show for us. The restaurant was part of a private club which included several restaurants and bars, an indoor swimming pool, golf driving range, and courts for badminton, and tennis. I learned that Jyi-fong frequented the driving range, and Anny played badminton in a league. Maintaining the large complex must be expensive, I thought, and I judged the real estate alone to be valuable. It was an impressive facility.

Aiming to introduce their guests to modern Taiwanese culture, after dinner they took us to KTV. Karaoke TeleVision. We had never heard of karaoke but found that it was a popular pastime in Taiwan. People took lessons to improve their skill singing to the words of popular songs streaming on a television screen.

"You really don't want me to sing," I cautioned. It would be embarrassing for me. "I truly cannot carry a tune."

The Shens laughed.

"She's not kidding," L.A. said.

Julie patted my arm. "It is fun. You will sing."

I laughed, too, but nervously anticipated the moment when I would have to perform. It would be no laughing matter then.

The complex of private Karaoke rooms for rent was a fantasyland. There was a huge, brightly lit KTV sign flashing above the center building, which we entered to find ourselves in a large hotel-like lobby. Anny registered our group and we proceeded out the rear door into a manicured garden ringed by assorted cottages

Anny and Jyi-fong

to accommodate different size groups. In the convenient shop, Anny purchased drinks and snacks from a selection of treats unfamiliar to us. Well supplied, we settled into our private cottage, consisting of a single large room and a bathroom. A comfortable circular sofa faced the huge, mounted television and two microphones wired into the wall. This would be fun, I kept reminding myself.

We chose songs from the selection book and punched their code numbers on the television's remote control. When the words displayed on the screen, Jyi-fong burst into song. Julie had told us that he was good, but that was an understatement. Whether singing in Chinese or English, he sounded like Elvis. Anny and Julie were also excellent. The Train men were passable, and I sang as badly as I had warned. Despite the Shens' kind assurance, we knew there was no hope for any of us.

It had been a wonderful day, and though I was physically tired, I enjoyed writing my journal, re-living the highlights of our trip so far. My toilet fiasco, the factory tours, seeing the Shens' home and family, the food, our personal Elvis impersonator, and especially meeting my new friend Anny. I settled in bed and couldn't tell when the memories became dreams, as I looked forward to what tomorrow would bring.

The next morning, we returned to Winton Tile for further meetings until time to catch our flights. In a small conference room, Julie translated the business discussions between Jyi-fong and the Train brothers. After finding a place for me to work on my own project, Anny went to her desk in the open office space several people shared.

As our company's Total Quality Manager, I facilitated team workshops to streamline processes and procedures. While the Trains and Shens met, I planned to use the time to prepare for the next month's sessions. I settled in a back room at a large table with three of the Winton Tile office staff who were entering information in ledgers. The two young women and one gentleman industriously attended to their work, until one made a comment, and they all took a break. There were many comments and many breaks that allowed chattering, laughing, and friendship. I enjoyed their joy even though I didn't understand a word they said, and the morning passed quickly. About the time I wondered if lunch was on the agenda, Anny brought in take-out food. I prided myself for my improved chopstick skill and Julie noticed, too. Congratulations were in order.

As we were scheduled to fly to Taipei about 8:00 p.m., the pace of the business discussions quickened to finalize negotiations before our departure. An employee returned from an errand and rushed to speak with Jyi-fong. "There is a storm coming," Julie translated. "This girl says she drove through it and it is very bad."

We saw that the skies had indeed darkened. Soon the

tempest erupted, and with thunder and lightning we lost power. What was simple inconvenience to me was disastrous in the factory, ceasing all production on the Swiff-Train order that was in process. The plant foreman brought in two battery-powered floodlights and the meeting continued, but soon it was too hot without air conditioning. Julie said, "Jyi-fong does not want you to be uncomfortable. We will leave here."

We watched for the weather to subside a bit and drove to our hotel's restaurant to continue the discussions. When the bountiful dinner buffet opened, Anny and I automatically switched to mother mode to take care of our families. We joined the swarms of diners and filled plates for our men and Julie so they could eat while completing their agendas before flight time.

We raced to the airport in two cars, Jyi-fong driving L.A., Kenny, and Julie so they could continue working out loose ends between our two companies. I rode with Anny and most of the luggage. Maneuvering through rain and heavy traffic, we arrived with a few minutes to spare before departure. While the men handled our luggage, Julie went into the small airport to check us in, quickly returning to report that all flights were grounded due to the weather but might resume later that night. We all took a moment to think, unsure what to do.

"You can leave us here and we'll wait for the flight," L.A. told Julie.

"Not yet," she said. We Trains observed the Shens

rapidly speaking in their native language, and it was clear they were in agreement. "The plane might not leave tonight," Julie said to us. "You will stay here and go tomorrow."

That made sense to us, as the skies were dark, and the rain had not abated. We agreed to remain in Tainan and fly to Taipei the next morning. Thus, the Shens, who thought they were almost done shepherding three foreigners, had to maintain their energy and carry on one more night.

Julie had tirelessly translated from English to Chinese and back again, while Anny and Jyi-fong had labored to converse with us directly. They must have been exhausted. Nevertheless, the Shens could not have been more gracious. Standing outside the airport under an awning which provided minimal protection from the misty rain, Anny went to work. On her cell phone, she efficiently cancelled our Taipei hotel reservations, found available rooms in Tainan, and contacted our morning appointment to reschedule for us. Meanwhile, Julie took care of booking new plane reservations.

After reloading all the baggage, we proceeded to a different hotel. An unexpected challenge loomed when Jyi-fong's alternator failed, leaving his car without lights in the darkness of the rainy night. Always a demolition driver, he now had to drive defensively. Anny and I followed closely in hopes her headlights could help him, and we all prayed that his battery wouldn't drain completely before he could get the car to a mechanic.

Stressed but safe, we gratefully checked into the new hotel and told our hosts good night. L.A. put his hand on Jyi-fong's shoulder and spoke directly to him as Julie translated. "You guys are tired, and we appreciate everything you've done, but you don't have to worry about us. Tomorrow we will take a taxi to the airport."

They wouldn't hear of it, and in addition, insisted on another night on the town. We had only an hour to rest.

"Do we really want to go out again?" I asked Kenny and L.A.

"No, and neither do they, but they're so hospitable that we owe it to them."

"Right," Kenny said in agreement.

We quickly freshened up and were ready on time. They took us to the third floor of an office building with several rooms for small groups, as well as a restaurant which prominently featured a piano. The host greeted Jyi-fong and Anny warmly and seated us on stools around the piano, which served as the table. We ordered drinks, Anny selected snacks for us to share, and we sang along with the pianist. Kenny was enjoying the dried squid until he made the mistake of asking what he was eating. None of us inquired again.

We were surprised when the pianist packed his music

and left, to be replaced by a fresh musician. "What's happening?" I asked Julie.

"They play for one hour and then change clubs. The customers like to hear a variety of performers every evening."

"Don't they waste time driving from club to club?"

"This area is full of them. There are five in this building alone."

It was becoming clearer to me that the Taiwanese worked hard and played hard. Karaoke microphones gave the increasingly inebriated and uninhibited patrons a chance to be entertainers. Julie and I discovered the deceptively powerful Long Island iced tea, a mixture of many alcoholic ingredients which tasted delicious. By the end of the evening, she was a prima soprano performing a rendition of Summertime from Porgy and Bess worthy of Broadway. Kenny and L.A. sang better than the previous night, and I was as bad as usual, but not even I cared. Jyi-fong performed several duets with Anny, until his latent Elvis persona launched into nonstop renditions of the King's hits along with repeated toasts to us. It had been a special day, a memory that even Long Island iced tea did not obliterate.

Refusing to leave their guests unattended, the Shens drove us to the airport early the next morning. Even though it was still raining, the planes would fly, and it was once more time to say goodbye. I expected to see

Julie frequently in Texas and possibly Jyi-fong at trade shows, but when would I have another visit with my friend Anny? This beautiful woman now occupied a special place in my heart.

We clung to each other, hugged many times, and declared we would miss being together. It would be five years before we hugged again.

CORPUS CHRISTI
approximately 1999

The Shens were coming to Texas! Jyi-fong and Julie planned to meet with L.A., Kenny, and Swiff-Train Company sales management in our Houston branch, now our largest facility and central distribution warehouse. I was honored that Anny was willing to ignore jet lag to travel to see me in Corpus Christi on the only full day they had in Texas. Fluent in English due to her education in Canada, Betty would accompany her mother and translate for us.

Anny's one day in our city promised to be just enough of a visit to leave me wanting more of my friend, but I was happy for the time that we would have. I vacillated between excitement at seeing Anny and doubts that only one day would allow enough time to reciprocate the hospitality she had shown me. I deliberated, thought about the limited time and the many things I wanted to show her, and revised the itinerary again and again. I appreciated our memorable experiences in Taiwan and the effort she must have put into planning for our visit.

The Shens flew from Taipei to Houston the previous day, giving them time to recover somewhat from jet lag before seeing us. Their 9:00 a.m. arrival in Corpus Christi required Anny and Betty to allow two hours to drive from their hotel to the Houston airport in morning traffic and check in for the short thirty-minute flight.

"Thank you for coming to my home town," I said as I welcomed my friends with warm hugs. "You must be very tired."

Anny thought for a moment and spoke to her daughter. Betty turned to me. "My mother said that you are worth her being tired."

Betty was now a beautiful young woman and her proficiency in English allowed easy communication among us. Arm in arm and shoulder to shoulder, Anny and I walked to my car, which was parked in the almost empty lot at the airport exit. There was no hustle or bustle of frantic travelers, no crowds to navigate. She seemed surprised when we quickly arrived at our Swiff-Train Company warehouse, which was only ten minutes away on the same street as the airport. It had to be clear to her that Corpus was not at all like the metropolises of Houston or Tainan.

After a quick tour and introductions, we left Swiff-Train. Our next stop was our home, which I knew would not be impressive compared to her marble floored garage and ivory museum, but it was important to me for her to see our natural habitat. We had lived for over twenty years in the one-story ranch style house nestled on a quiet street inside the doglegs of a country club golf course. The children and pets had moved on, and we were empty nesters. "Do you miss them?" Anny asked. Her son Winston was on tour with a rock band, hoping to find success as a singer and drummer, but her girls still lived at home, as did the widowed Mr. Shen and his caregiver.

"We like it," I laughed. "It's wonderful when they visit, especially with the grandchildren, and it's just as good to have the house to ourselves when they leave." She smiled but made no comment. I had the sense that she was thinking about living with no one but your husband and how different that would be for her, though we didn't pursue that conversation.

I drove Anny and Betty to see Padre Island, the 113-mile narrow strip of land creating a natural barrier between the Gulf of Mexico and the Texas coast. We had begun yearly Train family reunions on North Padre in condos just thirty minutes from Corpus Christi. I explained the work my sister-in-law Marilyn and I shared to manage four generations together for a long beach weekend. We cooked and shopped and organized activities and enjoyed every exhausting minute.

Betty translated for Anny, who said, "I do that, too."

I chuckled. "With your big family, I guess you do that every day."

On the way, we talked about our two companies. Betty was becoming involved in Winton Tile; our Train family, too, welcomed our next generation into the business. Did we want our children to stake their futures on family relationships, or find their own paths? And how did a daughter who was already showing great interest and aptitude for business view traditional practices regarding sons? We had an interesting discussion but no answers.

I had made luncheon reservations at the Town Club, on the top floor of One Shoreline Plaza, the prettiest building in Corpus. The excursion took too long, and we had just enough time for a late meal before their afternoon departure for Houston. Anny complimented the elegant dark wood décor and admired the beautiful view of the treelined waterfront boulevard and sailboats in Corpus Christi Bay. Our sparkling city by the sea looked magical that day. We enjoyed the buffet, which was a very full lunch offering but not the extensive over-the-top array presented in Taiwan. We were in my city, so it was my turn to take charge of Anny. I made sure my guest tried every dish, and she seemed to like most of them.

During the fifteen-minute drive to the airport Anny appeared tired. She was probably still jet-lagged, and I recognized the effort it must have taken for her to understand our English conversations during the full itinerary I had planned. I escorted them through the check-in process and spent the last moments of their brief visit at the boarding gate. "I will miss you," Anny and I echoed as we hugged goodbye. It was a long and busy day for my friend, and we had not had enough time together.

The visit was over in a flash, unsatisfying for me because nothing had been fun. There had been no experiences, just a tour. With more time, we could have gone crabbing, or spent a few hours at the beach. Perhaps taken a stroll on the bayfront. I had tried to fit in too much and suspected I had not succeeded in giving her a taste of our life. And to make matters worse, I had no idea when we would see each other again.

From time to time, I remember that day and think that I should have met her in Houston for a more leisurely visit, but I chide myself. I can't change what was.

I wanted my friend to see my way of life; perhaps she got a glimpse.

SURFACES TRADE SHOW
January 2005

I didn't see Anny again for almost six years! L.A. and Kenny had made several trips to Taiwan, but there was no business reason to include me. I didn't feel that I missed an opportunity to see my friend during that time, however, because Anny was seldom home.

Many Taiwanese families sent their teens to Vancouver, Canada, for high school and college, allowing them to attain English fluency along with an excellent education. The Shens had bought a condominium there for their children Betty, Connie, and Winston, located among friends from Taiwan, and Anny divided her time between her husband in Taiwan and their children in Canada.

We lost contact during those six years, but not our connection. On her trips to Corpus Christi, Julie often brought me something from Anny. When he traveled to Taiwan, L.A. carried presents from me and returned with a gift from her. I treasured each item, knowing that she selected it with care. I took these presents to be a token of our personal friendship, and also an expression of her family's regard for our family. To me, the delicacy, uniqueness, and beauty of Anny's selections reflected her own characteristics.

Shopping for Anny required thought and a discussion with L.A. Her taste was as exquisite as she was, and I tried to choose gifts she would like. I wanted her to think of me when she looked at or used our presents, as I did hers. I still display many in our condo and seeing them each day brings me thoughts of my friend. An interestingly marbled and polished stone is the focal point of a braided tassel which graces a lamp. A tiny, frosted glass water lily floats on a cube of smoky green glass on our hallway display shelf. Signed in Chinese by the artist, a unique sculpture worthy of a museum greets our guests from its place of honor on our foyer console.

I valued the relationship the many gifts represented and cherished Anny's presence in my home but worried that our choices would not be as meaningful to her. Since Anny and I think so much alike, for years I just used my own taste and preferences as a guide and purchased something I myself would love to have. The graceful Franz vase would also be stunning in our own home, and the necklace was so unusual and stylish that L.A. agreed I should have one, too. It was challenging to find the perfect gifts for Anny and imagining her pleasure upon opening them gave me joy.

By 2005, Betty had replaced Julie as our Winton Tile

contact. She was in her twenties, completely fluent in English, and already knowledgeable about Winton Tile. A beautiful woman with a natural air of confidence and sophistication, Betty accompanied Jyi-fong to the annual Surfaces trade shows in Las Vegas. Her father was still the decisionmaker, listening to her translation of the discussions and telling her his response to relay to L.A. and Kenny. Our son Jonathan and nephew Jason had joined Swiff-Train, expanding the relationships between the Train and Shen families.

To me Betty was also my relative, like a niece, and it was heartwarming to observe the friendship developing between her and our boys. She had let me know that her mother could attend Surfaces 2005 if I would, too. Of course, I would, and was thrilled to see my friend once more.

Our Swiff-Train Company contingent arrived in Las Vegas the night before the Shens, and I had arranged to meet Anny at 11:00 the next morning. Our two families were staying at the Venetian Hotel, adjoining the expo venue, the Sands Convention Center. It was an exciting moment when I saw the elevator doors open to reveal my beautiful friend. The surge of joy I felt was reflected in Anny's look of recognition followed by a smile that spread from her mouth to her eyes. I rushed to her as she hurriedly walked toward me, and with a warm hug we celebrated our reunion.

"I have missed you," we echoed. I have many friends, but somehow my relationship with Anny is different. I sensed our spiritual bond and felt a connection as if we had known each other before we met. In other places, in other lives. I was happy to find that the years in Vancouver had been educational for her, too, and we were able to converse without a translator. Speaking slowly and distinctly still was necessary, but a barrier to our communication was now minimized.

"My family wants to see you," I said, and we automatically linked arms, leaned shoulder to shoulder, with heads almost touching, and walked the long hallway to the convention center. I enjoyed the now familiar custom, cherishing our strong connection as we navigated the aisles to the Swiff-Train exhibit.

When lunch beckoned, we found a rare table and chairs near a food counter and paid exorbitant prices for sandwiches and chips. I talked about my children and grandchildren, Anny repeated my words, and I confirmed that yes, that is what I said. Our process reversed as she described her Vancouver experiences. The conversation continued until we agreed to return to our hotel and browse the shops.

We rode the Venetian escalators to their version of Venice, complete with properly attired sailors steering gondolas on canals. The replicated San Marco Square featured high-end boutiques with commensurate price tags, and we browsed. Anny's disinterested perusal of the exquisite jewelry told me we had reached the same conclusion. There was nothing we were going to buy.

"Let's go," I said, and she nodded in agreement. We walked into the square. "I wonder what's going on," I commented as I noticed people standing in clusters with their backs to us.

Anny pointed and said, "It's something there."

Together we peered around a group blocking our view and saw that everyone was watching living statues. Anny and I looked at each other with smiles, acknowledging our delight at the unusual sight. We stood for a moment to observe the young woman dressed in a diaphanous white goddess costume standing on a pedestal, her exposed skin covered in white stage makeup. She was immobile, as any marble statue should be. No blink of an eye, no twitch of a finger, no sway or movement at all. At the same time, we both turned our heads to see two people stand up and walk away from a bench. Without speaking about it, we took their seats. Anny and I silently watched in awe, focused on detecting any lapse by the statue. After at least fifteen minutes, the goddess suddenly turned, stepped off her perch, gathered her tips from the pavement, and walked away. A male gladiator dressed and painted in patina green took her place.

I was so fascinated that I hadn't noticed Anny yawning. "You are tired," I said.

"Yes."

Even with jet lag, she had given up sleep to spend time with me, and I felt terrible that I had been so insensitive. We agreed that we would meet again for dinner, and she rushed away. Her haste increased my guilt.

By that evening, Anny was rested and energetic, and I loved her stylish outfit and perfectly chosen accessories. It felt like a family reunion as two generations of the Shens and Trains mingled. When our group took seats, Anny and I automatically sat together. She moved our chairs so that we could be closer, and we leaned toward each other to keep our shoulders touching. It gave me pleasure to explain the menu items to Anny, reciprocating for the times she had done the same for me. I learned it was helpful to ask Betty or her fiancé Jason Shu for the exact translation. It was fun to be her hostess, and the menu discussion led to talk of recipes and wedding plans.

"You know we will be there," I said.

"Yes."

"Is there a date yet?"

"No." At my questioning look, Anny said, "They are very busy."

"Whenever it happens, we will be there."

"Yes." With nothing more to say, we dropped the subject.

During dinner I noticed she shared my plate. To me, that intimacy was an example of our close connection and I was honored and comforted to have such a friend. It was lovely to be so in sync with Anny, and to think she felt the same. I appreciated being cared for and cared about, and the conversation around us was so lively that no one else seemed to notice our eating arrangement. The only item missing was chopsticks. Photos from that evening show a happy and congenial group.

Anny and me

Our time together ended the next morning when the Shens left Las Vegas for Canada to visit friends, but I wasn't sad. I was going to Taiwan with L.A. and would see her in just two months.

TAINAN March 2005

L.A. and I departed Corpus Christi on a Friday at 7:00 a.m. We didn't make our tight connection in Tokyo and had to take a flight to Taipei instead, find a hotel room for the night, and fly to Tainan the next day. After traveling twenty hours, we didn't care what city we were in. Our only goal was to find a stationary room and sleep on a bed. We had crossed the International Date Line, lost a day, and were exhausted.

After sufficient rest followed by a typically bountiful hotel buffet, we flew to Tainan Saturday afternoon. Betty and Anny met us at the airport and brought us to the elegant Tainan Landis Hotel for a welcome rest before dinner. While Betty drove and conversed with L.A., my friend and I sat in the back seat, nestled against each other and happy to be together again so soon after the Las Vegas expo.

"You look wonderful, Anny," I said. "You have excellent taste." It took several exchanges for me to convey that I admired her sense of style. Not only does she choose fashionable clothes and accessories, but Anny is also beautiful, with the slim figure to make any outfit look even better. I envied her sensible eating habits, in contrast to my own constant fight to maintain an acceptable weight. Food seems to speak to me, and I too readily answer, whereas Anny naturally stays in perfect shape.

Despite her apparent self-control regarding food, Anny always entertained and fed us well, and planned a full schedule. The Shens hosted dinner at a fine French restaurant, and we ordered our choices by the set. In other words, diners selected from pre-set courses with no substitutions allowed. We played it safe and took Anny's recommendations. The first beautiful dish placed before me looked like it might be a shrimp curled around some other tidbits. I tried to be discreet as I examined the appetizer in case I needed to remove the shell before eating it. By 2005, my husband had made several trips to Tainan and had experienced many exotic dishes. "Don't ask," he advised when he saw my confusion. "Just eat." Whatever it was, the dish was delicious and not at all crunchy.

Friends of the Shens with their ten-year-old son were in the restaurant celebrating the boy's birthday, and the young man was obviously interested in us Americans. He was polite and intelligent, enthusiastically speaking with us in excellent English. The scenario could have taken place in Corpus Christi, as we often saw friends at restaurants, but I doubted if a child in our city would be able to converse in Chinese. It was a sobering and impressive experience.

We would have been grateful to return to our bed in the Landis Hotel after dinner and catch up on sleep, but Anny's itinerary for the night had not ended. We hurried to leave the restaurant in time for our 10:00 massage appointments, though Jyi-Fong was allowed to go home. Betty, Anny, L.A., and I first had foot massages for an hour, then body massages for another hour. The men who were assigned to each of us were strong, and though Anny taught me the word for "softer," mine didn't stop hurting me. Betty and Anny were dozing and didn't seem to notice my pain, and L.A. was unsympathetic. When it was finally over, I felt looser and noticed that the mean man had gotten out the kinks from those long flights. Bedtime was about 1:00 a.m.

Betty and Anny picked us up much too early at 8:00 a.m. Sunday morning and drove us to the Winton Tile factory. Anny had engaged a small bus and driver for an excursion to a famous forest about two hours north. Along with a few of the Winton Tile staff and their children, we boarded the bus and waved goodbye to Jyi-fong as he returned to overseeing the factory. Betty informed me that there would be important and interesting stops along the way. As was every experience with the Shens.

I noticed that the road was ascending, and Anny confirmed that the forest was on a mountain. After about an hour, we stopped to visit a tea museum. Betty had pointed out the dense, short tea plants covering the sides of the road, a special variety grown only in that area.

Anny as always was in charge of me, and with linked arms and shoulders touching, she escorted me through the exhibits. The museum displayed drawings depicting methods of growing and processing tea leaves, and Anny translated the signs to help me understand the procedure. I was fascinated by the ancient equipment and tools used for harvesting but was not clear if they were replicas or actual artifacts. With somewhat bent and rusted metal, they certainly looked authentic.

The museum was small, with limited scope. I was so fascinated that I wanted to learn more about the history of tea in Taiwan and later researched to find additional information. Because of the island's strategic location, Taiwan has been occupied and ruled by a series of aggressive conquerors. In 1602 the powerful Dutch East India Company was granted a monopoly on all forms of trade from the Cape of Good Hope to the Straits of Magellan, as well as sovereignty over any land it occupied. Identifying Taiwan as a profitable source of products and a valuable location to base their trade with Japan and China, the Dutch ruled the island, governing almost every aspect of life. Introduced to tea by their Chinese trading partners, the Dutch found wild tea growing in Taiwan but were expelled from the island before a viable tea industry could be developed. Their influence remains in the government systems they initiated, schools they established, churches they built, and laws they created.

The island came under Chinese control about 1683 during the Qing Dynasty. Anny's family left China for Taiwan toward the end of this dynasty, possibly to escape the civil unrest in their country.

During this time, many single men migrated to Taiwan and married aboriginal women, gaining the right to travel and work in the mountains where wild tea grew. By the early 18th century, cultivation spread to additional regions to meet China's demand for tea. Forced to open ports to international trade following the Opium wars, China allowed Taiwan to increase tea production to fulfill the growing demand and establish other industries to export new products. Throughout the world today, Taiwan is respected as a reliable supplier of goods.

Japan ruled Taiwan after the Sino-Japanese wars in the late 18th century, further increasing the tea industry by adding new varieties. Twentieth-century industrialization shifted focus in Taiwan to manufacturing, though today the Taiwan government actively supports the growth and development of their tea industry.

The museum exhibits emphasized the difficulty and effort required to produce a cup of tea, and I appreciated the progress made in that industry over the centuries. The shift from farming to industrialization allowed families like the Shens to establish factories and related services, and Anny's grandparents to develop a catering business. Like the Trains and my own Chafetz family, her relatives started with nothing, found opportunities, worked hard, and prospered. Anny and I share that heritage.

The last exhibit was the museum's shop, which offered tea sets, envelopes of the region's tea leaves, books about tea, and snacks. Betty and Anny purchased a packet of the local tea for a later tasting, chose enough treats to feed several busloads, and then led us to vendors outside the museum. Tiny dates simmered in pots of syrup, and the smiling sellers happily gave us the many packages our hostesses purchased. The small dates were soft, with tiny seeds, some sweet, some more savory, and all were delicious.

For the next hour, L.A. and I enjoyed the refreshments, dozed, and watched the scenery as our bus climbed the steep road. We parked in a lot at the entrance to the forest, and Anny pointed to the restaurant where we would later eat lunch. It was already noon, and I was glad she had supplied snacks.

This was no primitive site. We entered a well-planned attraction with wide, paved, slightly steep paths winding through the tall trees and lush undergrowth. The Shens had advised that Julie and her husband Eric were coming from their California home to spend time with us in Taiwan, and we were delighted to find them waiting for us. We had not seen Julie in several years, and it was a fond reunion. She looked slim, beautiful, and happy. They had driven to the forest with the senior Mr. Shen and his caregiver. Anny told me that though his wife had died since our last visit and he needed dialysis three times a week, at 79 Mr. Shen hiked in a forest the other four days. He seemed fit and energetic, and I concluded that the caregiver's primary job was to be a companion.

On this clear cool day, there were hundreds of visitors walking or hiking through the forest, but no other Westerners as far as I could see. As we strolled arm in arm, Anny and I comfortably chatted in our slow and distinct manner and laughed at ourselves as Mr. Shen briskly passed by and left us far behind

We completed the circuit back to the entrance, and Anny announced that it was exactly the right time to keep our restaurant reservation. We had walked for about an hour and a half, and I looked forward to a chair, a meal, and a restroom. Additional memorable experiences were sure to come.

First I visited the restaurant bathroom and appreciated the familiar western style accommodations, then stood at a sink to wash my hands. A girl I judged to be Taiwanese and no more than 10 years old seemed unsure how to turn on her sink's faucet, so I reached over and did it for her. She turned to me and with a sweet smile, said, "Thank you." I was amazed. Another Taiwanese child already knew English at such a young age, and furthermore knew that this foreigner spoke that language. Not French. Not Russian. My amazement turned to guilt in the knowledge that I would never be proficient in her language.

Betty assisted Anny in keeping my plate full, and it was an enjoyable meal sampling the many dishes offered on the table's lazy Susan. These ever-present round revolving trays placed in the center of dining tables were an efficient way to serve large groups, and my caregivers made sure I tried everything. I was especially intrigued by the stuffed bamboo. Stalks split in half the long way were filled with a meat and vegetable mixture, the halves tied together and steamed. It was an unusual woody taste, but not my favorite. I answered her unspoken question when she looked at me and indicated she would put another serving on my plate. "It's interesting," I said, "but I've had too much to eat already." That was the truth.

The ride home was relaxing, though I was glad when we stopped for a break at a coffeehouse. The best treat happened a little later when we parked along the sidewalk of a small town where a huge metal pot stood on a tripod over an open flame and delivered tantalizing aromas. Anny bargained with the vendor and treated her guests to one of the most delicious delights I have ever had: baby sweet potatoes fresh out of the cauldron of simmering molasses. It was a taste I would never forget.

"Be careful; they are hot," Anny said as she handed me a small plastic tray and a fork. The tiny, peeled yams had absorbed so much of the sweet syrup that it was like eating sugar. Just thinking about the sinful indulgence still brings back the taste, the aroma, and the memory of that wonderful day.

It was late afternoon when we returned to the Tainan Landis Hotel, and we begged Anny to excuse us from dinner. We had been on the go and fed all day and had no desire for another meal. Her quick agreement confirmed that she was exhausted, too, and we hugged goodnight.

Betty drove us to the Winton Tile factory the next morning and I sat in on the intense business discussions between L.A. and Jyi-fong. Julie was present but left it to her niece to translate skillfully and patiently, and I noticed that Betty had become more of a participant in the process than simply conveying the men's words to each other. She offered opinions and solutions. This young woman was impressive, and I enjoyed observing her.

Just when my hunger indicated it was mealtime, Anny appeared with a large steaming pot and assorted serving dishes. My friend was not only beautiful, but also an accomplished cook. She had prepared a beef soup with fat chewy udon noodles and repeatedly filled our bowls, watching us savor the unique flavors. Her smiles showed pleasure in our enjoyment, and she encouraged us to try the salads and small accompaniments. When I asked about the recipe, she patiently explained the ingredients and instructions so that I could treat my friends to an authentic Taiwanese dinner. I jotted notes and imagined the fun it would be to bring a bit of Anny to Texas. A few weeks after my return home I received a fat envelope in the mail. It was from Julie. She had written the recipe in English and included a packet of the star anise Anny thought I would not find in Corpus Christi. I was thrilled and once again overwhelmed by the thoughtfulness and consideration the Shens showered upon me. I named the soup Anny.

We had to leave Winton Tile after lunch for an hour drive with Betty and Jyi-fong to the Kaohsiung airport for our afternoon flight to Shanghai and the Domotex expo in Hanover, Germany. Too soon, I had to bid goodbye to Anny. I expected to see Betty and her father in Texas and at trade shows, but once again wondered when my friend Anny and I would meet again. She promised to visit me in Corpus Christi, but I couldn't depend on that. It was up to me to get myself back to Taiwan.

2006

Julie had traveled to Corpus Christi many times since 1994, meeting with L.A. and Kenny, staying in our home, and cooking with me. Our families had become good friends and I was sorry when she retired from Winton Tile to pursue other interests. However, I gained a combination niece, granddaughter, and friend in Betty. When she and Jason Shu planned to marry, I gained another relationship with the Shen family. This handsome and intelligent young Taiwanese man had been educated at a United States business school. He was a perfect partner for her and a valuable asset to Winton Tile. The couple were both tall, svelte, and beautiful. I saw them at trade shows, and often they came to Corpus Christi. I was honored when Betty presented gifts to me from Anny. She explained her mother's reason for each selection, often saying that Anny has one and wanted me to have one, too. A tassel for my purse. Colorfully embroidered inserts for my sandals. A Franz porcelain sculpture. I felt Anny's friendship and thoughtfulness in each item and cherished the love they expressed.

Setting a wedding date did not seem to be an urgent concern for the Shens, as the couple proclaimed they were busy with their Winton Tile responsibilities. We made it clear that we expected an invitation and would attend.

Betty explained the traditions. "The bride's family hosts an engagement party and the groom's family gives the wedding several weeks later. You will come to ours." Both formal events would include hundreds of guests. On one trip to Houston, Betty spent productive time at Neiman Marcus, and we expected that the engagement was imminent.

TAINAN December 2006
The Wedding

The engagement celebration was scheduled for December 17, 2006. Kenny, Jonathan, L.A., and I would attend. We received instructions.

"My Mom will wear a long dress and heavy jewelry," Betty told me. "You should wear a long dress and heavy jewelry. And you will make speeches...all four of you." It was a tall order. There would be 500 Taiwanese guests who might or might not speak English. L.A., Kenny, Jonathan, and I practiced our short presentations and hoped the Shens did not expect them to be in Chinese.

During the event's formal meal, it was customary for the bride, groom, and their parents to parade through the crowd on an actual red carpet, the bride wearing a different outfit for each of the five walks. Betty's trip to Texas to conduct business with our family coincidentally – or specifically – gave her an opportunity to buy gowns and accessories. I was excited to see what she had chosen.

We four Trains arrived two days early. Because it would be formal with so many guests, I thought of the event as a wedding, though it was called an engagement party. Anny told us that the celebration was a matter of tradition rather than religion. No ordained officiant or house of worship would be involved, and the marriage would be signed and sealed at the court house at a later date. Anny conveyed that the most import objective was to observe their customs. I thought of my own desire to honor my heritage by continuing customs which have no religious mandate. The blessings would be as valid said over a store-bought slice of bread as I believe they are when we pray over my homemade challah. And what other than tradition dictates that for our Passover Seders we serve the same menu as our grandparents enjoyed? Tradition means a lot to us all.

We had one full day in Tainan prior to the event and spent it at Winton Tile. As if they did not have a major occasion looming, Betty and Jason were not at all nervous, working at their factory and carrying on meetings with us as if it were no big deal that they would soon make their union official. I sat in on the discussions rather than invade Anny's last minute tasks.

Both evenings before the important day, we enjoyed congenial dinners with the Shens, including Julie and her husband Eric, in from California, and Anny's grown children Winston and Connie. Julie now operated a Christian day school, Winston was pursuing his dream of a rock and roll career, and Connie had a job separate from the family business. Feeling like part of one combined family, we Trains were as happy to celebrate the bridal couple as the Shens seemed to be. Anny and I naturally sat close together as she kept my plates full, answering my questions about what tomorrow would bring. First there would be a gathering at their home, with the formal lunch to follow at a hotel.

We laughed about Betty's directive that we give speeches, but I assured Anny. "Don't worry about us," I said. "Thanks to my mother, I'm not only ready but looking forward to it." My mother enjoyed public speaking and wisely sent my brother and me to a series of elocution lessons so we would be comfortable in front of an audience. Thanks to Mama, I was confident and undaunted by the prospect of addressing 500 guests. It promised to be a joyous event, and I took my friend's hand. "Anny, we are honored to share the engagement with you. Thank you so much for including us."

She smiled, thought for a moment, and said, "Good for you to be here." Her body language spoke more than the words, as she covered my hand and we both smiled with excitement and joy. It was a memorable time with my friend. We retired after the early dinner and looked forward to the next day.

Mr. Wu drove us to the Shen home at 9:00 a.m. for the first event of the day. I had donned my long formal dress and heavy jewelry and my three guys were handsomely attired in suits and ties. We entered through the garage as always, to find that two long tables lined the space along the sunken fish pond. A groom's table and a bride's table displayed gifts from each family to the couple. Betty received heavy and expensive gold jewelry, set with diamonds, emeralds, and other gems. The fur and leather vest was stunning. The Shens gave Jason a set of golf clubs, membership in a country club, gold bars, and a watch. There was more, all indicating the two families' regard for each other. I had seen gift tables at bridal showers or in a bride's home, but nothing as impressive as this. I observed the guests as they perused the display with approving smiles and nods, and I concluded that these two families were well respected.

As promised, Anny was breathtaking. She wore a long gown, fur wrap, and heavy jewelry. Her tall, exotic-looking daughter resembled a fashion model of the highest caliber. Their men and Connie were also in full dress, and it was evident that the family had given much thought and time preparing for this day of celebration. The guests, however, were a mixed group. Several Buddhist monks wore their normal golden robes, and many young folks came in blue jeans and t-shirts. The older generation dressed primarily in what Texans would call church-appropriate outfits.

We were proud that the Shens treated us as honored guests and included us in many photos. Their guests smiled and nodded to us, and those who spoke English acknowledged that they had heard there would be American friends attending. Everyone gathered for the presentations, and filled the space near the gift tables, lining the stairs, and leaning over the mezzanine railing.

The Shens welcomed everyone to their home, formally presented their gifts to Jason, and Monks blessed the couple. The agenda continued with the description of the process which introduced Betty and Jason. A mutual friend knew both families and thought their children would make an excellent pair. This determined woman took charge of the introductions and monitored the progress of the romance, and proudly and publicly took full credit for the success we were celebrating that day. I had to agree with her that she had facilitated an exceptional match. Most of the speakers kindly made their presentations in English. If not, someone translated for us.

That was it, until the engagement luncheon scheduled for two hours later. We returned to our hotel, changed into nap clothes, and rested until time to leave for the party, a formal lunch at a different hotel.

Now everyone was in sync... the men wore suits and the women were in elegant long formal dresses and heavy jewelry, draped with furs, sparkling with diamonds, and exuding glamour. Gift tables overflowed with large, wrapped packages, and gentlemen handed red envelopes to the groom. Red is the traditional color worn by Chinese brides, as it is believed to ward off evil and signifies luck, joy, and happiness.

The Shen guests laughed and visited with friends as they streamed into the large ballroom of the fine hotel and found their places. Fifty round dining tables flanked the length of the red carpet, with ten place settings and a gorgeous flower centerpiece on each. A stage and huge screen waited for us at the far end. It was an elaborate and stunning setting, and I was both excited and impressed, filled with joy for our friends, and proud to be part of this special event.

Betty, Jason, and the parents made their first grand entrance and paraded on the red carpet. All 500 guests stood and applauded the happy families. This repeated a total of five times, with Betty wearing a different dress for each walk. The most outstanding of the fabulous creations was the red one, the striking color emphasizing the joy of the occasion. I felt one with the assembly as we transmitted good wishes for the beautiful couple's health, joy, and long lives. Betty and Jason's ceremonial walks cemented a great partnership. L.A., Jonathan, Kenny, and I were honored to be there.

Anny had thoughtfully placed us at a table with English-speakers: Julie Shen and her husband, a niece who was married to a Brit, and another business-related couple. Conversation was friendly and primarily involved a discussion of the menu. It was a many-course lunch and the waiter kept my wine glass full, so I tried to pace my food and wine consumption. Since some of the dishes suited my palate more than others, it was hard to determine if I should fill up on the ones I liked, or just take my chances. All in all, I remember being busy with my chopsticks constantly in action and my fork at the ready just in case, enjoying our camaraderie with the Shens and their friends.

We were greatly honored when Jyi-fong took to the stage and delivered a speech, first in Taiwanese and then in English. It helped that the words streamed on the screen in our language. Only the Trains required English, and our hosts had gone to a lot of trouble to make it easy for us to understand.

Betty had warned us, and thus we were ready when it was our turn to climb the three steps to the stage. Kenny, L.A., and I spoke briefly and well, I thought, and by their smiles and nods, the Shens indicated their appreciation. My advice to Betty involved what it's like working with your husband and trying not to talk about business at home, even though that will be impossible. That got a laugh from the audience as the guests translated for each other. Our Jonathan, however, was the star. He ended his short presentation with bows accompanying the Chinese word for congratulations, *gongxi gongxi*. The crowd was delighted, and his mother was proud. Several of the guests warmly greeted us in English or Chinese and indicated that they had enjoyed our remarks. Anny hugged me and with big smiles said we were good. It had been a memorable and joyous event and Anny seemed happy with our speeches, which made me happy.

Everyone was exhausted, and I welcomed my late afternoon nap.

But it wasn't over. Our gracious hosts insisted on taking us to dinner that night, and the next day we returned to the factory to finalize more negotiations, specifications, and orders. No wonder our families are such close friends and associates…we both live by my father-in-law's philosophy: if you take care of the business, the business will take care of you.

TAINAN December 2013

Left to right, Jason, L.A., Jyi-fong, Betty, Anny, and me

We cruised on Celebrity from Singapore to Hong Kong and added a few days to see our Winton Tile family in Taiwan. Our destination was Kaohsiung, and we expected that the Shens would send a driver to transport us the distance to Tainan. It was an exciting and heartwarming surprise to see them waiting for us. All of them. Anny, Jyi-fong, Betty, and Jason. My heart leapt and I'm sure my smile and whoop let them know I was thrilled. I couldn't get to my friend fast enough. At sixty, Anny was as beautiful and shapely as ever, and in her fashionable slacks and blouse and tasteful jewelry, more stylish than I have ever been. L.A. and I hugged them and thanked our friends for being there.

"My mom insisted we meet you here in Kaohsiung," Betty said. "She couldn't wait to see you."

Anny smiled and nodded in agreement as we easily resumed the Chinese custom that is so comforting to me, naturally linking arms to walk. We piled our luggage and ourselves into their large van, and Anny and I nestled together on the back seat. Shoulders touching and heads cocked toward each other, we chatted in our slow way to catch up on the seven years since we were together.

They took us to a Japanese restaurant in a high-rise building with a beautiful view of Kaohsiung. It was only lunch, but on the griddle at our table the chef ceremoniously prepared at least five courses. To honor our hosts, L.A. and I were obligated to consume them all. Regardless of the early hour, we joined Jyi-fong and toasted each other with wine and beer. Anny as always took charge of me and plied me with food, and I noticed that Betty was second in command of my meal. With the two of them adding bits and bites to my plate, I was concerned that the Taiwan trip combined with my cruise indulgence would result in a tragic homecoming. None of my clothes would fit. I chose to worry about it later.

Betty and Jason had departed from Chinese tradition and lived in a condo rather than in the Shen home with Anny and Jyi-fong. That was acceptable to Anny until their son Ryder was born. At that point, my friend cleverly solved the grandmother issue by convincing Jyi-fong to purchase the condo next door to the young family. That way she could be an everyday part of her grandson's life,

Anny wanted to tour a condominium building in Kaohsiung to see model units by a decorator they had heard about. I love construction, too, and we enthusiastically talked about the buildout process in Taiwan. Only the exterior and delineating walls would be included in the purchase price, with the interior completed at additional expense. Buyers usually hired a decorator to design the architecture and décor, and this was an opportunity for Anny to see the highly recommended man's work.

The first protocol in viewing the showcase condos was to remove your shoes. This was a custom which we had not previously followed, and I wondered if the Shens were too polite to ask us to do that in their home. But the rule in the sparkling new condos was clear, and we added ours to those already in a line by the front door. The three units were ultra-contemporary, lovely to visit but not my taste. Shiny metals, glass, dark woods, contrasting white floors, and the best appliances and fixtures did not make up for what Anny and I agreed was a poor use of space. I noticed only one small oven in the kitchen area and learned that most preparation is done on a cooktop or in electric woks or skillets.

Dumplings and bakery products are purchased. They rarely use ovens. With my love of cooking and baking, this was definitely not the dream home for me.

We all seemed tired and ready to board the van for Jason to drive us to Tainan. Anny and I settled in the rear seat and continued to discuss the condo, until we agreed Jyi-fong had the right idea. He was asleep in the front passenger seat. Anny and I dozed for a good part of the hour, while Betty and L.A. talked nonstop.

Anny allowed a short time for us to check in to the hotel and rest before dinner, but we suggested that we all get a good night's sleep to be ready for the next day she had in store for us. Our hosts readily agreed, and our relaxing evening of room service dinner while watching *Forrest Gump* was just what L.A. and I needed.

Anny and Betty picked us up about 10:00 a.m. and took us to the Being Spa at the Tai Landis Hotel. Anny went to the women's area for a massage. She told me there were private rooms and a large comfortable parlor with beautiful views where she often spent the day relaxing with friends after massages.

Jyi-Fong had booked the honeymoon suite for L.A. and me to have a couple's massage. I prefer to separate, as L.A always converses with his masseuse and I like to zone out. We knew our host had given us a generous gift, so we agreed to suffer this luxury. L.A. and I relaxed and even napped during the experience and enjoyed the two hours. We dressed, drank tea, and ate sweet bean soup in the ante-room, and waited for Betty and Jason to pick up Anny and us for lunch.

"Your son Jonathan loves this place," Betty told us as we walked into the busy restaurant. "He said we must take you." We loved it, too. Although the large storefront was filled with people dining in or ordering takeout at the counter, we were able to find seats at one of the Formica-topped tables reminiscent of my grandmother's kitchen. Numerous varieties of dumplings, soups, and other Taiwanese lunch dishes were served to share. I think all Asian dishes are intended to be shared. My chopstick skills had improved, and I didn't even notice that there were no forks. After eating our fill and more, we were ready to do a little sightseeing when Betty said, "Jonathan always drinks fruit juice after lunch at this restaurant. We are going to the juice stand."

"I can see that our son is directing our itinerary," I said with a laugh, but was glad that he and Betty had developed such a close friendship. We walked a short distance to the corner, where the busy women did a brisk business at their counter open to the sidewalk. I had a mango drink, which was simply the perfectly ripe fruit blended with ice. I sipped it all afternoon, thinking I would enjoy mango freezes back home. Anny called Mr. Wu to meet us, and we boarded the van for a historical tour.

"Anny wants you to understand our history," Betty translated.

"Very important to Taiwan," Anny said. In contrast to the busy commercial streets we usually saw, the Tainan Confucian temple, built in 1665, was a serene and graceful complex of buildings. Ancient Confucian ceremonies were still conducted there on a regular basis. Renovated many times over the past 300 years, it was surrounded by beautifully manicured plantings and trees so old and large that one required the support of many cables and posts.

Anny and Betty waited in the souvenir shop while L.A. and I explored the small temple. Open doors leading to the pagoda revealed a massive wall with the teachings of Confucius written in calligraphy. A friendly English-speaking Taiwanese gentleman was seated in the only chair and watched us trying to decipher the information placards. He leisurely walked to us and in a friendly manner explained the meaning of the characters. We thought he might have been a guide stationed there to assist tourists, but we didn't ask. Perhaps he was simply a nice man who enjoyed helping others.

As we left him, L.A. and I discussed our grasp of his explanation that whereas Buddhism is a religion, Confucianism is a philosophy which can be related to any religion or way of life. Our instructor's unique English pronunciation challenged our understanding, but the sense was that a person and even a culture can be compared to a tree. The roots must be strong for the trunk to be strong, and without a solid base the branches cannot be sustained. We concluded that a person must respect himself, keep his priorities straight, work for harmony in his world beginning within himself, and extend these principles to his family, his society, his government, and his environment. Who could disagree with this?

Anny locked her arm in mine as we walked to meet the Winton Tile van, and I thanked her for the visit. "We enjoyed seeing this beautiful temple and we learned about the teachings of Confucius."

"So different," she said.

"Not so different," I said. "The lessons for living a good life are the same in every religion."

"Be a good person. Take care of your family."

"Exactly," I said. "That's all it's about." We rode in comfortable reverie to our next stop, the Chihkan Tower.

In 1625 Dutch colonists bought a piece of land in southern Taiwan in exchange for 500 meters of fabrics. From that beginning they briefly ruled Taiwan, as we had learned at the tea museum. They built businesses, marketplaces, warehouses, and hospitals. After an uprising against them in 1653, the Dutch built Fort Provintia, also known as the Chihkan Tower, to serve as their administrative center. In 1662 they were driven out by the Chinese Ming Dynasty, which had lost control of China and sought other land to dominate. Though destroyed by earthquake and deterioration, the Chihkan Tower had been restored as a museum and national historic site. We enjoyed the brief visit to this beautiful setting.

Anny and Betty had one more surprise for us. "You will like this," Anny said as she guided us across the street to a shop.

"I smell something familiar," I said.

"Sugar and peanuts," L.A. identified.

"This is Taiwan style," Betty said as we perused the display of peanut candy.

"Taste this," Anny said again and again. I sampled all three types. She sent me home with a box of the two I liked, so that I could share another Taiwanese specialty with my Texas friends.

I thought Mr. Wu was taking us back to the Shangri La for a short rest before dinner, but Betty said, "We will make two stops before your hotel." She went into a building and we waited in the van while she picked up 2-1/2-year-old Ryder at his school. We could meet him for the first time.

When he ascended the step into the van and saw me, he was more than shy, I think actually frightened, and averted his face in rejection. As they climbed into the rear seat behind me, Betty spoke to her son in Chinese, urging him to acknowledge us. But Ryder turned to face the back window and refused to even look at me or be seen by me. L.A. was in the front seat and out of his line of sight, but I was too close. Not only were we strangers, but we also didn't look like the people familiar to him. Though she spoke in Chinese, I knew Betty was telling him we are Uncle Jonathan's parents. Even that information didn't comfort him. By the time we arrived at the factory, though, Ryder was warming to us. With his back to me, he sang Jingle Bells. I joined in the chorus, and he continued singing. He even stole a few guarded peeks. When we arrived at Winton Tile and everyone but L.A. and I left the van, Ryder quickly waved goodbye and ran away. I thought that was progress.

While the family housekeeper drove Betty and Ryder to their home, Mr. Wu took us to the hotel. We dozed on the ride and looked forward to a proper nap before he returned to take us to meet the Shens at a restaurant.

At dinner we visited with Jyi-fong and Anny's son Winston, who had been learning the business for seven months, and daughter Connie, now an English tutor. Jyi-Fong honored us again by arranging for us to experience shark fin soup, an expensive and special delicacy. This was my first taste, and I loved it. What I thought were noodles were shark fins. To me they were crunchy with little taste, but I especially liked the squid and vegetables, as well as the broth itself. Adding wine vinegar made it even better. Enough is never enough, and again the food kept coming. I ate a little bit of everything, and noted that in this restaurant, too, we were the only foreigners. We love experiencing life with the people who live there.

Betty drove L.A. and me to the Winton Tile factory and quickly hustled me to the van. Mr. Wu was waiting to drive me to meet Anny. While business discussions occupied our family at the factory, Anny and I would spend the morning together elsewhere. We were the designated lunch chefs and needed to buy ingredients. I thought we would go to a supermarket and then cook in the family home. Instead, Anny introduced me to the traditional market in a large one-story building with crowded narrow aisles. Booth after booth of local vendors sold the freshest food for that day's consumption: steaming fresh cooked corn; raw fish, poultry with the heads and feet, and meat; fruits, vegetables, dumplings ready for cooking, nuts, spices, vacuum packed fish eggs, and even clothing. The place was packed with buyers and sellers, but Anny led me

Anny purchasing steamed corn

by the hand to her favorite stands and answered my questions regarding the unknown foods I saw. She also fielded questions about me, posed by locals who were surprised to see a foreigner in their midst. I received curious stares and was quite the topic of conversation.

With our bags of groceries, Anny and I took a taxi to their condominium building so we could cook in their condo where Winston now lived. There was their housekeeper, Marina, already prepping for us. In fact, Anny gave her all our groceries and she prepared the entire meal.

Anny and Jyi-Fong's condominium was beautiful, elegant, extremely contemporary and a stark contrast to the Shens' traditional family home. The open kitchen, dining and den area was quite modern, but showcased many of the elder father's ivory and statuette collection. A beautiful wood and mother-of-pearl inlaid game table and chairs from their family home added a lovely touch of tradition.

Because the open kitchen would allow cooking smells to permeate the condo, there was an adjoining full kitchen similar to an enclosed porch, separated from the rest of the unit by a door. This was where the action happened. Marina tended a fish soup in progress, containing mussels, shrimp, squid, the local fish Anny had invited me to sample in the market, onions, pieces of unsweet doughnut-type dough, and I'm not sure what else.

While waiting for the family to arrive, Anny and I

snacked on the fresh steamed corn and dried lychee we had bought at the market, as well as unshelled macadamia nuts. Because their shells are as hard as coconuts, Anny had bought a bag with them slightly sawn and a little metal handle which had a point to insert in the slit. The idea was to twist the handle to crack open the shell so you can capture the nut. Anny said she had bought the small augur because it looked interesting. We agreed macadamia nuts were worth the effort, but we preferred them from cans.

While we waited, Anny brought out her mahjongg set, and I showed her the version we play in my neck of the woods. She was amazed. "So different," she said. She laid out the tiles and I agreed that it is a totally different game from the one she enjoys.

"Jason can teach you," she said, and we hoped that there would be time for him to educate me.

L.A., Jyi-Fong, Betty, and Jason arrived about 1:00 p.m., with Ryder in tow. He ran to me with open arms saying, "Grandma!" I took advantage of his big hug and interested him in opening macadamia nuts while he sat on my lap.

I looked to Betty and asked, "What changed?"

We laughed when L.A. said, "He's 2-1/2." That explained it.

Betty said, "I don't know why, but when he woke up this morning he told me that today he would hug

Grandma and Grandpa." The rest of the visit, the handsome and energetic Ryder played near me, brought me items to see, and made me feel like his real grandmother. So being Uncle Jonathan's parents paid off as always.

We sat around the large family dining table and enjoyed the wonderful lunch Anny and I had not prepared. The soup was divine, not at all fishy tasting, subtly flavored and served boiling hot. We also had minced meat balls served on braised cabbage, smoked chicken which Anny had purchased at a neighborhood shop, and a dish like quesadillas filled with Chinese spinach. Dessert was fruit. In the market, Anny bought one which I had never before seen. It was thick skinned, a very lumpy bright green, and reminded me of the size and shape of a hand grenade, of all things. You break off the lump, which has a moist, lychee-like covered seed nestled within, and you eat the pulp as well as the sweet pudding-like substance at the base. Delicious and like nothing else I knew.

Our visit was coming to an end, and we remembered to take the presents out of the car. Anny and Betty seemed to like our gifts, but I could tell that Ryder was waiting for his. I felt terrible that we hadn't thought to bring anything for him, but he was happy when I surprised him by popping the bubble wrap and showed him how to do it.

During our few days in Taiwan, we had taken hundreds of photos to document our visit, so we posed for the last few. With hugs and thanks, we took our leave of the Shens. I promised Anny I'd return to Tainan soon.

INTERIM YEARS

December 22, 2014, we sold Swiff-Train to an equity investment company who wanted our family to continue working. I was happy to have a place in the company and gratified that the new owners encouraged me to maintain a presence. Our son Jonathan became President and CEO. Jeffrey's son Jason maintained his position sourcing products in Asia. No longer executives, the Train brothers and I focused on our major strengths. L.A. and Kenny concentrated on international sales, and Jeffrey fulfilled operational functions that no one else had yet assumed. My role facilitating teams diminished as others handled process improvement.

Already in my seventies, I was content with the reduced responsibilities and enjoyed more free time to do whatever I wanted while still maintaining a presence in the business. Many of our personnel called me "Mom," and I cherished my position as a component of the family culture we and the new owners wanted to maintain.

I considered retirement but was torn between two ideal choices: staying or leaving. I loved being part of our business. I loved my co-workers and I loved that they loved me. I loved feeling important. I loved feeling needed. I loved being the only person who knew or could or would do something. But if I retired, I could write the books I was determined to publish, travel more, and spend more time with friends. I wasn't ready yet, but with Jonathan's encouragement I began writing and we scheduled land trips and cruises. And we included a few days in Tainan for a visit with our Winton Tile family.

When the Shens came to Houston to meet with Jonathan, Jason, and their team of decision-makers, L.A. was still involved in the discussions. Betty and her husband Jason made several trips, and we Trains hosted them as we would any of our own family. After Winston joined his father and sister in the Winton Tile business, he traveled to Houston with his sister and brought his fiancée Alice. They stayed at a hotel just a few blocks from our condo, and we enjoyed bringing them to our home. The visits became meetings, as there is no time off in a family business.

After dinner on one trip to Houston, Jason Shu experienced severe symptoms of intestinal distress. L.A. took him and Betty to an emergency clinic, where they administered an IV and sent him home. Immediately in maternal mode, I tucked him into our guest bed, and he slept for hours. While Betty and L.A. talked, I made congee according to her instructions and occasional oversight. I loved congee for breakfast in Asia, along with a variety of condiments, and learned that the rice gruel is the cure for digestive issues, with the same holistic properties as chicken soup. He was able to eat a little bit, and as he settled under the covers for another nap, he thanked me for going to the trouble for him. I love taking care of people, and Jason was now one of my children. Plus, I had added another remedy to my motherly repertoire.

Tall, handsome Winston and his beautiful Alice were delightful and loving additions to our life, and on their first trip to Houston I reminded him of his indoor skating exhibit years ago. With a playful grin, he assured me that he became proficient and his father loved watching him.

On Sunday Betty chose to spend the afternoon with us, her surrogate grandparents, while Jonathan took Jason Shu, Winston, and Alice to an Astros baseball game. She and L.A. have a special bond and wanted to spend time together, and I planned to cook dinner for everyone, so we took a field trip to HEB grocery. It was fun to compare our choices to the market fare I had seen with Anny. I believe Betty's talents and interests lie in her business involvement, not especially in the kitchen, and she seemed to enjoy perusing the frozen and fresh prepared meals. She laughed when I passed up the boxes of pasta and bought a roller attachment for my mixer so I could make my own. While I was as happy as could be in my kitchen making lasagna from scratch, Betty and L.A. were in the den, deep in serious conversation. We three had a lovely afternoon and so did the baseball fans. That day everybody won.

We ate a family dinner at our dining room table as Shens and Trains devoured my lasagna, everyone chatting and laughing, so comfortable being together. I was as proud of Betty and Winston as I was of Jonathan. I thought Anny and I had achieved the highest goal possible – we had raised our babies to be fine adults who had chosen perfect mates.

TAINAN March 2017

During L.A.'s phone conversations with Betty, I occasionally inquired about her mother. Her responses never varied. "Anny misses you. She wants you to come to Taiwan again."

"I would love to!"

"Then do it!" We always laughed because it wasn't happening, but one time Betty added, "You know L.A. will be here after Domotex Asia. You should come with him." L.A., our son Jonathan, and several associates now attended numerous international trade shows to market our vinyl tile, including this yearly March event in Shanghai.

"I'll think about it," I said. The more I considered the possibility, the more I was determined to do it.

The Swiff-Train contingent planned to spend two days in Taiwan after Domotex, and L.A. encouraged me to meet him there. "You could spend time with

Anny before I arrive. It would be nice to see you in the middle of my three-week trip."

That made up my mind for me. If my husband of fifty-five years wanted me to travel halfway around the globe so he could see me, who was I to deny him the pleasure? Betty confirmed the plan with Anny, and L.A. and I worked on the itinerary. My excitement was greater than my uneasiness about following the complicated plans.

A master of plane reservations, my husband explored numerous options, then purchased my ticket for a flight leaving at 1:00 a.m. from Houston to Taipei. I frequently traveled alone, and occasionally had braved foreign airports and transportation to meet L.A. in Paris, Brussels, and Tokyo. I even made my way through New York City. But there was always someone who spoke English. It would be an understatement to say I was apprehensive about traveling to Tainan alone, but I really wanted to see my Anny.

So, on a Wednesday night, about 11:30 p.m. I took an Uber to the Houston airport and checked in along with the rest of the sleepy passengers. My next step was to exchange money at the airport, where the rate is better than local banks, but the service was closed until the next day.

"Don't worry," a man told me when he noticed me standing in front of the sign with a distressed expression, "it's cheaper in Taipei."

Reassured, I followed the stream of people to the lounge and dozed while waiting for the plane's delayed departure. After sleeping intermittently during the sixteen-hour flight, I arrived in Taipei at 5:15 a.m. Friday morning, coherent enough to identify my luggage and breeze through the minimal entry process into Taiwan. With relief, I spied the currency exchange window and saw that it was open. It took just a few minutes to buy New Taiwan Dollars (NTD) at a more favorable rate than my home bank and the Houston airport offered. The man who had reassured me passed by with a thumbs up, and I smiled a thank you.

I faced the tricky next step: taking a taxi to the train station. There is more than one train station, I knew from my research, and I also had been warned that taxi drivers do not speak English. So, I asked the currency exchange clerk to write a note in Chinese for me to give to the taxi controller, who would explain to the driver that my life was in his hands. She graciously did so, and I was relieved to have that communication ready.

I found the person who seemed to be in charge of the taxi line and handed him the note. He nodded that he understood and gave the message to the driver, who nodded at me that he, too, understood. I could only hope so. We loaded my suitcase and carry-on bag into the messy trunk of the dusty car, and I settled on the least sagging expanse of back seat. As the driver sped along the deserted streets, I again briefly wondered if my body would ever be found but chose not to worry about something out of my control. I leaned my head back against the seat and tried not to think about insects possibly infesting my hair or the taxi careening into an embankment at its current warp speed. I dozed until we turned into the train station drive. The driver gave me change for the NTD bill I handed him, and I had no reason to doubt that the station and the change were correct. I mentally checked off that step in the plan to get Ronarose to Tainan.

Impressed with my success so far, I confidently rolled my luggage and found my way through the modern and immaculate building to purchase a first-class ticket for the next train to Tainan. I was relieved that one of the cashiers spoke English and listened carefully to her instructions for reaching the boarding location. She pointed, and I followed her finger, repeating to her what I needed to do. It involved taking a specific elevator down to the track for the train heading south. That one, down, south. I got this. I set out with less confidence than I had felt only minutes before, but I had at least twenty minutes to get to the track, enough time to blunder about until I got it right. A confused look on an obviously foreign face at 6:15 a.m. attracted pity, and several people graciously stopped to help me, even though I didn't ask. None spoke English. A woman kindly escorted me to my platform, and I thanked her in smiles, nods, and one of the few Chinese words I know, *shi shi*.

Betty's husband Jason Shu was to meet me at the Tainan station, but we weren't sure which train I would be able to make. Even though it was only 6:30 a.m., I thought it a good idea to let him know. I realized that my phone was foreign to Taiwan and I needed to tap in their country code. I didn't have it. "Could you help me?" I asked a young woman in a glass-enclosed office on the platform.

A very sleepy Jason answered the call. "Don't worry," he said. "I will be waiting for you in the station." And he hung up as I was thanking him.

It's such a pleasure to ride the high-speed trains everywhere we travel. They are clean, quiet, comfortable, and always exactly on time. I wonder if the United States will ever catch up with the rest of the world. The ride in the premier train car was relaxing, with few passengers. Most were dressed for business. I assumed they were commuting for an appointment in Tainan, as they quietly worked or used the time to doze. I read and took a short nap during the two-hour trip.

A smiling, handsome Jason greeted me as I exited the passenger area. "We are going to see Anny," he said after our hug. Then he laughingly added, "Thank you for calling me this morning, but I only went to sleep at 5:30."

I was mortified. "I didn't know," I said. "Why?"

"I was at Domotex, too. I flew home last night so I could pick you up this morning."

What a wonderful guy, and what a lot of trouble I caused. "Oh, Jason," I said as I patted his hand, "I could have taken a much later train."

"Oh, no," he smiled, "Anny wants to see you as soon

as she can."

My guilt was overshadowed by joy and anticipation. Anny and I were going to have a great time and I couldn't wait to see her!

"Where are we going first?" I noticed that my body had no clue what time it was, and suddenly felt very tired. "I should probably check in to the hotel and take a nap," I added.

"Anny is waiting for you," Jason said apologetically. "She told me to take you straight to her house."

I smiled as I remembered the cure for jetlag that I'd endured on many trips. Whether in Europe, Asia, or New Zealand, seasoned travelers swore to me that it's best to stay awake as long as possible until normal bed time. That practice usually helped my body clock to adjust, but it was cruel. On one visit to our Belgium office, I finally lay down and slept on the floor between my colleagues' desks. They laughed at the sight but took me to my hotel.

"That's fine," I said to Jason. " I napped on the plane, dozed in the taxi, and caught a few winks on the train. I can make it for a while."

While driving, Jason filled me in about the Domotex trade show, and I asked about their son Ryder. "He must be about seven now. Where does he go when you travel?"

"Home. His Nanny stays with him. You remember Marina, right?"

I did. "She's Anny's housekeeper."

"Ours, too, and takes care of Ryder."

"And Anny is in charge of the Nanny, right?" We laughed, but I knew the truth. Anny had no intention of leaving her grandson to a caregiver while his parents were away. "Ryder is lucky to have such a devoted grandmother, and you're lucky you don't have to worry about him while you're gone."

He nodded agreement as he turned into the familiar street. My excitement quickened as Jason called Anny on his phone, and then the garage door opened to reveal my friend walking toward us. My eager smile mirrored hers, and we rushed to embrace. After a long and tight hug, she led me through the door into her home and held my shoulders as she examined my face, then slowly turned me around. She nodded, smiled, and said something in Chinese.

Jason translated. "She says you still look the same."

"So young," Anny said.

We all laughed as I protested. "Not young, but you look as beautiful as ever." I had concluded after years of being exposed to several Asian cultures that the highest compliment for a woman is that she looks young, whereas to me, telling Anny that she is beautiful is high praise. I realized I should use her criterion rather than mine, and slowly and distinctly said, "You look young, too. You do not look like a grandmother."

She took a moment to consider my remarks and with a broad smile and a nod, said, "Thank you." Anny picked up her purse and announced, "Now we will have breakfast."

I was so happy to be with Anny that when she took my hand to lead me to Jason's car, I didn't ask for a few hours to rest first. "Sure," I said, "I can always eat."

We drove to a bustling street with a grassy roundabout on one side. A stately tree grew in its center, providing shade on that sunny day. I was impressed that the city valued a tree enough to save it. Jason expertly drove into a spot that was magically available among cars and mopeds parked at odd angles by the roundabout. Anny went to the take-out counter inside a small storefront while Jason and I secured a table on the sidewalk. It was perfect weather to dine outdoors, just cool enough, with sunny skies. Pleasant aromas wafted from the boxes the steady flow of customers carried as they rushed past us. Judging from their attire, I identified laborers and office workers, and didn't envy young mothers tending babies in strollers. A few patrons, like us, leisurely enjoyed a meal al fresco. Cars and trucks slowed to maneuver around people walking and eating their way across the street. This was a popular place, the kind of gem known only to the locals.

"It is a typical Taiwan breakfast," Jason explained as I examined my bowl.

"I thought a huge buffet was typical," I said.

He translated my remark for Anny, and she laughed, saying, "That is only in hotels." She pointed with her chopsticks to my bowl. "At home we eat soup." We held the bowls to our lips and drank the broth, picking at the vegetables and pieces of fried fish. I followed their lead and popped grilled garlic cloves into my mouth between bites and slurps. Anny tore chunks of fried dough and dipped into the soup. It looked so good I didn't need more than one demonstration to do the same. I had enjoyed those breakfast buffets, but that was for the tourists. Anny was giving me an inside look at life in Tainan.

We wanted more fish, so Anny added to that item on the slip of paper showing her original order and went back to the counter. I was interested in her formation of the number and Jason and Anny gave me a lesson in the Chinese system. Unlike most Western languages, it is a logical progression of adding lines and symbols so that anyone who can count the lines and knows the few symbols can read numbers. I could do it that day, but not now.

I wish I had practiced. I wish over the years I had studied Chinese enough to have more than three words in my vocabulary. The language is so different from English in every way, but I could have accomplished a little. Anny would have been delighted and I would have been proud.

I remember a conversation I had with a British expatriate in Beijing when we attended Sabbath services. While chatting, I walked with him to retrieve his daughter from the children's room.

"Do many expats learn Chinese?" I asked.

"When you ask if one speaks Chinese, the answer is usually 'I have 2000 words.' Ask if they read Chinese, they say, 'I have 500 words.' But ask if they write Chinese, the answer is always 'No.' It's a difficult language." He nodded toward a girl on the floor with paper and pencil, writing Chinese. "You have to learn when you're young, unless you're very smart and very determined."

So that's my excuse.

After our breakfast outdoors, Anny and Jason finally took me to the Shangri-La Hotel to check in and rest for a couple of hours. I was delighted to notice a door in the lobby opening directly into a large department store. How convenient, I thought, and wondered why I hadn't discovered it on our last visit. But first things first. I didn't even unpack before settling into the very firm bed and sleeping deeply for an hour until my alarm rang.

I was refreshed and ready when Winton Tile's driver Mr. Wu picked me up to meet Anny and Jyi-fong for lunch at the starkly contemporary Silks Place Hotel. I admired the twenty-foot ceilings, dark woods, ancient-looking statues and wall art, open spaces with low chairs in subdued beige and grey. It was striking. Anny was waiting for us in the lobby. She and I linked arms to walk to the elevator, chatting in our slow and careful manner.

As we exited the elevator and proceeded toward our lunch location, I heard a deep voice singing, "Rona, Rona, Rona." Who else could it be but my personal Elvis impersonator Jyi-Fong. With a mischievous smile he continued the tune as we hugged hello and strolled to an exclusive dining room. I saw men in suits and women in business-appropriate attire seated at the few tables in the same subdued décor as the lobby. This setting was a contrast to our morning breakfast venue, and I appreciated the opportunity to experience both.

Jason joined us, saying, "Sorry I'm late. There were things I had to do at the factory."

"You have to be exhausted," I said.

He smiled as he settled in his chair and thereafter patiently translated as Anny, Jyi-fong, and I conversed. We would have had a difficult time conveying our thoughts to each other without Jason to help.

There was no menu because Anny had ordered a special meal. A waiter placed a small cauldron on our table, and the aroma of the simmering beef broth filled the air. He returned carrying a large tray with an appetizing display of raw vegetable slices, tofu, and tiny meatballs. Each of us received a plate of raw, thinly sliced beef. He added the tray's contents to the pot, we dipped our beef to cook to the desired doneness in the hot broth that was becoming a rich and delicious soup. Bowls of sauces, rice topped with minced meat in gravy, and as many plates of beef as we wished continued to appear on our table. Jyi-fong frequently toasted me, and Anny paid constant attention to refilling my plate and bowl. I felt special and honored, and also helpless, unable to resist the endless wine and delicacies. It was the beginning of a wonderful visit.

It was so nice of them to welcome me with that extravagant and memorable meal, and I thanked them profusely. We wandered into a hotel shop for a few minutes while waiting for the elevator, and I saw that it was a jewelry store. A unique titanium or white gold necklace with roses spaced on the chain looked just like Rona Rose, and it was obvious I liked it. Jyi-fong began bargaining with the salesman, but I couldn't let him buy it for me. "L.A. would not like another man giving his wife jewelry," I said, thinking fast. "He will be happy to get it for me."

For once, I prevailed, and intended to let L.A. know about the gift he could buy for me. Jason said, "Don't worry, Rona. We are coming back to this hotel. I will tell L.A." He smiled to assure me he understood.

Jason and Jyi-fong told us goodbye and drove away in their cars while Anny and I waited for the Winton Tile van. "My friend is coming," Anny said. "We are going to have a special afternoon."

As Anny and I met the Winton Tile van, the passenger door slid open and a woman stepped out. "I'm Rita," she said to me. "Anny and I have been friends for years, and she talks about you constantly."

Now I understood. Anny had apparently arranged to have a fluent English-speaker with us throughout my visit. Though she had improved her language skill over the years, she didn't have much practice between my visits and the next three days would have been tedious and exhausting for both of us without assistance. With Jason present, conversation had been easier for us all. Translating kept the darling guy busy, especially since he was already worn out. I recognized the care Anny had given to providing a wonderful memory for me. Rita's English pronunciation was excellent, and she quickly answered my unspoken question. "I married an American and teach English here in Tainan."

We boarded the van and I asked Anny as Mr. Wu drove, "Where are we going?"

"To the lace store," she said. "The. . . " She consulted with Rita for the correct word. "The seamstress will meet us."

"Anny told me she wants to give you a gift," Rita explained. "You'll select fabrics and Mrs. Chang will measure you for an outfit."

This was both good and bad news. "What fun," I said, and meant it, but knew that I would not be allowed to pay for the fabric and labor. It would be awkward if I showed too much enthusiasm, and it could be a more expensive gift than Anny might have planned. "I've never had custom clothes," I said. "It's going to be a memorable experience."

Inside the store, Anny introduced me to Mrs. Chang who was waiting for us, then I glanced at the racks of fabric bolts.

"She made this dress," Anny said, indicating the one she was wearing.

"It's fabulous," I said. "Of course, anything looks good on you!" It was a sophisticated brocade in shades of beige, cap sleeves, slightly flared to accentuate Anny's slender figure. Looking more closely at it, I saw that Mrs. Chang knew her business. "The fabric was a good choice for this design, Anny, and her seams are beautifully matched."

Anny reached out to me, clearly intending to guide me to the bolts of lace.

"Anny is ready to select fabric for you," Rita said, but the seamstress spoke up while waving her hands, unmistakably telling us to wait.

"She said you need to decide what you want before you choose the material," Rita said.

I saw that Mrs. Chang had pattern books on the table and indicated I could select from them.

Anny spoke and Rita translated, "Anny wants you to

have a dress like hers."

I had to reveal my shortcomings. "Thank you, Anny, but I don't wear dresses," I said, and with hand signs, I explained my short-waisted figure. "I look better with a tunic or long top over slacks or a skirt." Rita translated and everyone nodded their understanding. "Why don't we design a tunic for me."

Mrs. Chang looked closely at my body shape and turned me several times. Using hand motions and speaking Chinese, she made suggestions. Though we spoke different languages, she and I were in sync. After the wardrobe selection courses I took many years ago, I knew what looked good on me, and among the four of us we brainstormed. It was even more fun than I had anticipated, and language disparities didn't interfere with our creativity. I sketched, erased, revised, and accomplished a drawing we all liked. I wanted it slightly fitted to achieve some shape but since my own is well hidden by too many good meals, it shouldn't be too tight.

Anny and I began perusing the bolts of lace and selected a few to consider.

"Very good," Anny smiled in approval, and I had to agree. "You like this one, too," she said, indicating my second fabric choice.

Uh-oh, I thought, envisioning what would come next. "This will be beautiful," I said, indicating our lace and sketch. "I only need one special gift. My friends will already be jealous."

"I want you to make this one, too," she said. "It will be very beautiful."

Rita chimed in. "I believe she thinks you did not spend enough."

"Jyi-fong wants to buy more for you," Anny said.

Why should I argue? I didn't. I was excited to imagine our design come to life.

"This one is very nice," Anny pointed to a bolt we had eliminated. "You can have a jacket from this one."

"I can't thank you enough, Anny, but we are already making two fabulous pieces."

"I want you to have this, too."

Rita's expression encouraged me to say yes, but reticent to accept more gifts, I held out a while. Soon I had no choice but to yield. Designing that jacket and a shell to wear under it was the most fun of all. We four shared smiles and delight with a job well done.

Anny opened her purse, and I said, "Please, let me pay. You are doing too much for me."

"I want to do this," she said, and gave her credit card to the clerk. "They will be a souvenir. You will think of me."

As we carried our bags to the van, I thanked her again. "Of course, I will think of you, Anny. I will remember this day every time I wear these."

She smiled. "Yes."

We were quiet as we rode, and I mentally reviewed the details of my three tops. I hoped that when Mrs. Chang brought them to the hotel for a fitting the next day they would be lovely, but it really wouldn't matter. The experience was priceless, and I felt privileged to have such a wonderful friend. It was nice to have the moment for reflection, a break from the long day, and I relaxed. I noticed that Anny and Rita were stifling yawns, so I hoped that we were going to my hotel.

Not yet. Anny had planned another stop. We revisited Fort Provintia, the historical site now known as Chihkan Tower. L.A. and I had seen it on a previous trip, but this time we three were the only visitors that late afternoon. I admired the well-kept landscaping and graceful architecture of the several story structure, acknowledging that the Dutch had been sensitive to construct a building in the Tainan style instead of their own. "Our people didn't care what it looked like," Rita said. "They just wanted the Dutch to go home." We laughed. "But they left their reminders," she said, and then explained. "You can still see Taiwanese faces with a little Dutch in them."

We strolled through the building, and the ambiance was eerie. In the silence I imagined the days of long ago when from this fort foreigners protected their claim to

Formosa and assumed rule of a peaceful and industrious population which needed no rulers.

Anny held my arm to support me as we carefully navigated steep outdoor stairs with no railing. My hosts were tiring, as was I, and I welcomed Anny's remark. "Now we will go to dinner."

It was only 5:00 p.m. "It's early," Rita said, "so you will have a long evening to rest."

"It's been a wonderful day," I said to Anny as we boarded the Winton Tile van. "A perfect day." Her tired smile confirmed that she was happy her agenda had been a success. "Thank you for planning such a beautiful visit for me."

"I am so happy you are here," she said as we nestled into the comfortable seats.

Mr. Wu stopped on a busy street and we went into a tiny restaurant. As we chose one of the only three tables Anny said, "It's good to be early. In one hour, there will be a line." After explaining the menu choices, she ordered at the counter.

While we waited for our dinner, Rita translated the signs on the wall. "This restaurant is 123 years old. It is extremely popular."

The food was excellent, and after enjoying a light meal, we three agreed. It was time to go home.

"Tomorrow we will come to your hotel," Anny said.

"You will try the clothes."

"How can a seamstress make three tops overnight?"

Anny laughed. "Many people."

Rita added, "Her workroom is busy 24/7. You will have all three for your fitting."

We hugged goodbye and I gratefully headed for my bed and a good night's sleep. I'm sure Anny did the same.

Promptly at 9:30 a.m. as promised, Anny rang my hotel room doorbell. With her were Mrs. Chang and Winston Shen's beautiful fiancée Alice. We had met when she accompanied Winston to Houston, and I fell in love with her then. I was thrilled to see her smiling face and we rushed to hug. She is a rare combination of sophistication, intelligence, and sweetness. A dermatologist educated in China, Alice was not allowed to practice in Taiwan due to the political animosity between the two countries. She was now devoting her time to finalizing plans for the new condominium she and Winston would share.

"I will spend today with you," she said.

"That's fabulous news!" I said. "Did Anny tell you about yesterday?"

"Yes! I can't wait to see what you designed."

Mrs. Chang handed me one piece instead of three, the black lace top. It was gorgeous, and I was excited to try it on and model. The puzzled expressions on Anny, Alice, and Mrs. Chang's faces told me I was correct in thinking something was wrong. I knew what it was.

"Mrs. Chang doesn't understand why the bust is not right," Alice translated.

"'I'll show you," I laughed, and took something out of the laundry bag to reveal the culprit. "I was wearing this one yesterday." When the three women saw the full coverage bra I dangled in front of them, they burst into laughter. "I know this doesn't look like any of yours," I laughed with them, "but sometimes my ample figure requires help. I'm wearing a different one today, and maybe Mrs. Chang can measure me again." Otherwise, the piece was magnificent.

"She says that now she can make the others," Alice said.

"Anny, this is the best gift! You've made me so happy."

"I am so happy, too," she said, and arm in arm, we went to the Winton Tile van for the drive to our first stop.

Anny, Alice, and I spent the morning at the Taiwan History Museum. The building was large and contemporary, different from the graceful pagoda curves of the Chihkan Tower and other sites I had visited. The vacant surrounding property left room for future expansion. Though the museum had opened six years earlier, neither Alice nor Anny had visited it. We wandered among the life size mannikins in open settings depicting the island's history. Workers loading a small boat, a group demanding the Dutch leave Taiwan, a school. The museum's open exhibits gave us the feeling that we ourselves were experiencing that moment in time.

When we agreed that we had seen enough, Anny called Mr. Wu to drive us to her home. Jyi-fong and his son Winston greeted us there, along with Betty and Jason's son Ryder. He was now six years old, a beautiful boy with mischief in his eyes, and employed the same tactics as he had at 2-1/2: he pointedly ignored me. It was just us family sitting around the kitchen table, enjoying the delicious lunch prepared by Marina, the family housekeeper who also was Ryder's nanny. I didn't ask why he was not in school.

"These meatballs are wonderful," I said to Anny. "I remember you served them on my last visit."

"We call them lion's head," she said, lifting one with her chopsticks to demonstrate the shape. I wrote the recipe as she told me how to make them and added another Taiwan dish to my repertoire.

"Try this," Winston said as he observed the slippery noodles falling off my chopsticks on the way to my mouth. The twirl method he taught me helped considerably.

For dessert and tea, Anny directed us to the area by the now-empty sunken fish pond. We sat at their table that was sliced from the trunk of a native hinoki tree and highly polished to a shiny butterscotch finish. Jyi-fong proudly showed me that the creative use of the naturally irregular wood resembled the shape of an eagle. The seats were stumps of hinoki, so heavy that I had to ask Winston to position mine for me. Alice brought bowls of fruit and a box of cookies from the kitchen while Anny prepared for a tea ceremony. Ryder played with cars on the floor close by, still deliberately ignoring me.

"You're a wonderful uncle," I said to Winston as he spoke authoritatively but reasonably to Ryder in an effort to bring him to me. "I understand that I'm strange to him."

"He needs to learn manners," Winston said with a grin, "but he's really showing off for you."

I laughed. "I see that he now gets as close as he can, making sure I'll notice him ignoring me."

"That's how a six-year-old operates," he said. "He's warming up."

"I'm patient," I said, and took the cookies and serving of fruit Alice handed me.

"Anny loves to serve tea in the traditional way," Alice said while we sat at the eagle table and watched her. As I had learned in our 2005 visit to the tea museum, a cup of tea is not just a drink. The ceremony honors the guest, and the ritual gives the experience great meaning. Only the finest tea cups and pots made from the best clay can be utilized. Extreme attention is paid to the correct temperature of the water and the quality of the tea leaves. Anny poured boiling water over the dried leaves several times and threw away the first cups. "Now the tea is at perfection," Alice translated as Anny handed the first good cup to me. I carefully sipped the scalding tea.

"What is its origin?" I asked.

"Very special for you," Anny explained, and with Winston's help she related that this was from a region known for its rare leaves, unique drying process, and prized flavor. To add to the honor, she gave me the container of tea to take home along with the box of cookies. No protestations from me would prevail. It was a gift and once again I thanked the Shens for their generosity.

By early afternoon I was tired and welcomed the news that next on Anny's agenda was a massage. Winston and Alice took me to a spa where Anny had reserved two hours for me. My masseuse spoke no English, but she expertly worked away my knots and tightness. When I presented my credit card the staff laughed and indicated that the charges had been paid in full. Why had I thought otherwise?

Mr. Wu picked me up from the spa at 5:00 and when he dropped me off at my hotel at 5:30, showed me his hand. He had written "18:20." That's how I knew I only had less than an hour to make myself presentable before he returned at 6:20 p.m. to take me to meet Jyi-fong and Anny for dinner.

It was a seafood restaurant, and Anny quickly took me to the fish tank to select my entree. Rita again joined us, and said, "Later tonight I'm going to teach you our mahjongg."

"That's exciting news," I said. "I've wanted to learn the Chinese version for years."

Soon we were joined by Alice, Winston, Jason, and his son Ryder. "Betty has a cold," Jason said, "and she's already asleep." Though Ryder sat with his father far across the large round table from me, I caught the child stealing glances my way. To pique his interest, I employed his own tactic and carefully ignored him.

I did well handling my chopsticks to eat the delicacies Anny served me but didn't even try to lift a grey gelatinous blob that resembled putty sitting in a shell. It was not appetizing to me. Everyone laughed at my poorly disguised expression of dismay and laughed even more when Jyi-fong reached his plate out. Alice gave my mystery shell to him and he ate it with gusto. I had no idea what it was. Toasts and laughter were the order of the evening, and for me, the highlight was a toothpick.

My plan paid off when Ryder looked at me while whispering to his father. I heard Jason say, "Do it." After quickly running to me, Ryder looked away while handing me a gift: a toothpick. I was delighted that my patience was rewarded.

"Thank you," I said, and added, "could you unwrap it for me?" He carefully managed to peel the plastic sleeve off, still refusing to look at me as he gave it back."

"High five," I tried, and raised my hand for his slap. With his back turned to me, Ryder stretched his arm and offered it low. Everyone clapped as I tapped his hand in triumph. I couldn't see his face at first but did catch him grinning as he ran to bury his face in his father's lap.

Jason said, "He whispered that he wanted to give Grandma a toothpick."

That was great news. "Please tell him I'm honored to be Grandma again."

The conversation segued into what to do after leaving the restaurant. Jyi-fong's continuous toasts had been fun but the effects had made many of us tired. Jason agreed that with Ryder he would take his in-laws home. Rita was too mellow to teach mahjongg, and I was too mellow to learn. But Anny insisted I be entertained, so we agreed that Rita and I would ride with Winston and Alice and browse the department store adjoining my hotel. We could shop while walking off the dinner. That satisfied Anny and we said goodnight as we piled into our assigned vehicles. Once we drove away, I said, "Winston just take me to the hotel and call it a night."

"If that's what you want," Alice said. Everyone else indicated they were happy with that, and we parted after fond goodbyes.

As I walked to the lobby elevator, however, I saw through the glass door that the department store was still open. This might be my only chance to see what the store offered, and not wanting to miss an opportunity, I entered through the beckoning door. Before me was an interesting display. An extremely helpful and friendly salesman who was adorable with his spiked bleached hair and rock-star tight slacks introduced me to the unique products from Micanna of Italy. The company made leather furniture, and created interesting shoes, purses, and satchels using the scraps. The shoes were totally cool because a pair did not match. They were aesthetically pleasing together but different. And they were cushioned and extremely comfortable. After my purchase, falling asleep was no problem at all.

Our day began with an excursion to the Chimei Museum to see a visiting exhibit. Anny, Alice, and Winston picked me up at 10:00 a.m. to see the famous collection of origami, the art of folded paper. It promised to be an interesting morning.

"I have a confession," I said to Anny as I settled in the

car. "About last night." She had a confused look and I laughed. "The department store was still open, and I couldn't resist." I lifted my foot to show her, and she, too, was hooked. Alice loved my new shoes, as well, and we agreed that later we would make a visit to my salesman friend in the Micanna department.

Anny and me with Winston and Alice

Though it was cold and dreary, we posed outdoors for pictures with the beautiful building in the background. The philanthropic owner of Chimei Corporation built the museum to house his extensive collections of fine art, sculpture, armor, musical instruments, and more. The vast manicured grounds included a long narrow pond with a wide bridge, reminiscent of a moat. Carved marble sculptures on pedestals lined the walkway to the stately white building which, with its dome and columns, resembled a castle.

I was familiar with origami, as our Japanese customer Mrs. Shirihama-san had taught me to create birds when I spent time with her in Tokyo. I reciprocated by showing her how to fold paper to make boxes. But those were primitive compared to the intricate and creative designs we saw. We admired origami clothing, origami sculptures of faces and birds, and origami wall hangings. Each piece was a masterpiece in the art, requiring imagination and patience by the creator. "This is an amazing exhibit," I said to Anny as we wandered arm in arm and marveled at each piece. "I'm so glad you brought me to see it."

"Very special," she said.

"This visit is special," I said as she nodded agreement. "Thank you for everything you're doing for me."

We took the stairs to the mezzanine where Anny had made a reservation for lunch. The restaurant overlooked the museum lobby in one direction and offered expansive views of the grounds through the opposite wall of windows. The French décor made it an elegant space, with tone on tone wallpaper, crystal chandeliers, and Louis-the-something tables and chairs. Jyi-fong joined us for a leisurely meal and patiently listened to our enthusiastic description of the origami. I repeatedly glanced at the stairway, looking for Betty and Jason to arrive with L.A. and two Swiff-Train associates who were flying in from the Domotex trade show in Shanghai.

"They're here," Anny said, and I hurried to meet my

sweetheart. He looked tired after an intense two weeks in Asia. Our group greeted each other with hugs, then lingered in the restaurant, chatting as the latecomers ate. I was happy to be in L.A.'s presence and listen as he, Anny, and Jyi-fong conversed with Jason's translating assistance. Of course, I was unaware that Anny and I were about to experience a significant event in our friendship, the memorable exchange of coloring books. We walked out of the museum shop with our packages and for me, a new recognition of how similar we two were. I knew I would always cherish the true gift I had received there.

The sun had brightened the dreariness of the day by the time we left the museum, and reunion with my husband had done the same for me. In the car I showed L.A. my new coloring book, but he was too tired to show interest. Anny's afternoon schedule wisely allowed several hours for us to rest at our hotel, and I tucked my exhausted husband into bed for a long nap. By 6:00 p.m., we were refreshed and ready to meet Jason for the drive to dinner. Our son Jonathan had arrived in Tainan and I looked forward to hugging the grown man who was still my baby.

As a host escorted us to a private room, I observed busy waiters serving seafood to families in the casual atmosphere of a neighborhood favorite. "The food here must be very good," I said to Jason.

"This is a popular restaurant," he confirmed as the other patrons curiously glanced in our direction. After hugs all around, I took my seat next to Anny. The waiter placed a deep electric skillet on the table, poured in a little water, and emptied a bag of live prawns into it. He quickly placed the glass cover over the jumping crustaceans and turned on the heat.

"Very fresh dinner," Anny remarked as the glass began to show steam.

"As fresh as it gets," I said, cringing at the sound of the prawns hitting the cover, my eyes riveted on their diminishing activity as they succumbed to the steam. At first the process seemed cruel to me, until I remembered dropping live crabs into boiling pots, or relishing a rare steak. It's about the food chain. I joined everyone else as we peeled the hot prawns and enjoyed them along with the numerous dishes of soup, tempura, several fish varieties, and potatoes revolving on the lazy Susan.

Everyone was tired but instead of heading for the corral, we chose to have foot massages. For L.A., Jonathan, and our two associates, this was the third night in a row they had enjoyed that treat. Trade shows were hard on your back and feet, and that's only one excuse for indulging. The massage parlor was packed even though it was after 10:00 p.m., and all seven of us relaxed in luxurious recliner chairs and dozed while being creamed, exfoliated, kneaded, pounded, and rubbed. It was nirvana, especially because L.A. was there, too. All was right with my world.

Returning to tourist mode, I indulged in the Shangri-La's breakfast buffet with our Swiff-Train group, then went along as Betty's husband Jason drove us all to the Winton Tile factory. We greeted our old and new friends of the office staff in the common language of hugs, smiles, and nods. After a quick tour of the factory, I rode with Mr. Wu to pick up Anny at her home.

"What are we doing today?" I asked her.

"We will be with Alice," she said. "She will meet us at the condo office."

I was delighted to spend more time with Winston's fiancée. Her English is flawless, and I think she is, too. Beautiful, an accomplished dermatologist, and a sweet personality.

Anny explained, "Alice and Winston are working on a new condo."

I thought of the showcases we saw on the last visit, when Anny and I learned that we both love construction. "They have to design the interior, right?" Anny nodded, and I was excited to see the site.

"Very much work," Anny said. "You can tell Alice ideas."

"I would love to," I said. "I remember in Kaohsiung you and I thought alike."

Anny laughed, then surprised me. "Betty has one in

the next building."

"I'm sure Ryder needs more space now that he's almost seven."

"Their condo is not so big," she agreed as Mr. Wu parked the van in front of twin towers. "We will see the model first." We linked arms and walked to the building on the left, where Alice was in the sales unit intently conversing with the decorator. Alice and I spent the next hour discussing the merits of various features and options. Anny listened and occasionally told me that she agreed and previously had said the same to Alice and Winston. I gathered that the process had been going on for several months and the family had made many visits to this unit.

We walked to the next tower and entered along with construction workers bringing materials into the building. The marble floor leading to the elevator reserved for them was protected with plywood, and we waited for another, cleaner ride to the twentieth floor. The doors opened into a construction site. My kind of place. Alice explained their plans and again we delved into the details and possibilities while Anny listened and concurred. "This will be a wonderful home for you," I said. "A beautiful space for your growing family. I can't wait to return and see the finished product." I was happy for the young couple, and glad that children were included in their plans. I had observed their interaction with Ryder and expected that they would be good parents. Anny and Jyi-fong would have the pleasure of more grandchildren with the benefit of sending them back to their parents when enough is enough. That's what L.A. and I do.

We met the rest of our families and associates at the excellent and popular neighborhood dumpling restaurant we had enjoyed on our previous trip. The food kept coming and as always, our group consumed 99% of it. It was a perfect lunch. With our son Jonathan present, the next stop had to be the juice bar.

On the short walk to the corner, we passed a storefront that I suspected would have an item I needed, and asked Alice if she would help me. Jyi-fong joined us, too, and said, "NO, no, no." He brushed away my credit card and absolutely insisted on covering my purchase. The Shen generosity never ended.

The others left us to continue their meeting at the factory, and Mr. Wu drove Anny, Alice, and me to the Shangri-La Hotel. We had our own plans. First we were to meet Mrs. Chang to receive my new clothes. All smiles, she handed me the beautifully stitched tops and I modeled them for Alice and Anny. Mrs. Chang agreed with us that a few more tucks and tweaks were necessary and assured me that all would be perfect before I departed the next day.

Our next destination was the Micanna shoe department. My salesman friend was delighted to see that I had brought him more customers. We admired the purses and backpacks, then examined, discussed, and tried on every pair of shoes. We laughed to find that we three wore the same size, and each of us wanted the same pair.

"No problem," the happy salesman said. "I will get more for you." He explained that he would ride his moped to the two stores which had the inventory and meet me in two hours.

Anny insisted on paying for all of them, including another pair for herself similar to my first purchase. We could not carry on the battle of the credit cards forever, so I yielded once again and planned to reciprocate at the first opportunity. I chided myself for allowing yet more gifts, but I sure loved those shoes.

I bid Alice and Anny goodbye until dinner, and after they left me, I proceeded on my own to purchase a small suitcase for my new belongings. Exactly as promised, the perky salesman returned to meet me with the additional two pairs. Purple sandals with a huge leather rose on each shoe, on the front of one and on the side of the other. The same but different. So cool. Despite his moped tour around town, not a hair of his moussed and spiked coiffure was out of place.

When L.A. returned to the hotel, it was clear that he had a cold. He was too exhausted to join us for a special dinner in a private room in the Silks Place Hotel. I wore my new black lace top and toasted Jyi-fong and Anny in thanks for their generous gifts.

"So sorry L.A. is sick," Jyi-fong said as he proposed a toast to my husband, then to Swiff-Train Company, followed by Jonathan honoring Winton Tile. During the dinner we toasted each person in attendance. Everyone except Ryder joined the fun, and I was careful to drink only small sips of wine. I took the opportunity to honor Anny for being such a good friend and gracious hostess and thanked her for the unforgettable visit she had given me.

"This is a special dinner for you," Anny said. "L.A. will miss it." Our hosts had arranged a rare experience for us.

After several preliminary dishes which helped me handle the wine I was obligated to drink, a uniformed young woman wheeled a cart into the room, displaying a beautifully roasted duck. The aroma tantalized us as she explained its history in great detail, in Chinese. Winston translated for us. Born in Great Britain, the duck was imported to Taiwan and raised to be just the right weight, achieve just the right amount of fat evenly distributed, and have the honor to be our dinner. That duck provided six courses for ten people, beginning with crepes of the crispy skin with cucumber, water lily shoots, and sauce. Each dish was wonderful, and Anny kept my plate and bowl full. I enjoyed the camaraderie, the conversation, and the many toasts we made on our last night together. I missed L.A. but knew he needed the rest and room service chicken soup we had ordered for him.

Our son Jonathan raised his glass to speak for our company and thank our hosts Jyi-fong and Anny for the memorable evening. To be fair, we then toasted the duck who that night had given her all for us.

We walked to the elevator and passed the shop where I saw the Ronarose necklace my first day in Tainan. I had thoughtlessly mentioned it once since then, and Jyi-fong several times referred to my new necklace. Of course, I protested each time he mentioned it over the few days of my visit, until finally he said, "I insist. I-N-S-I-S-T." That evoked laughter from everyone at the table, especially because he professes he doesn't speak English well. I was embarrassed that I had shown any interest at all. The Shens are so generous that I wish I had kept quiet for once. If I can ever entertain Anny in Houston, I would love to reciprocate. Our dinner ended about 10:30 p.m. and to my relief as well as my disappointment, the hotel shop was closed. I hoped that no jewelry had been purchased for me and the topic was simply a way to have fun. But I sure had liked that necklace.

As late as it was, Mrs. Chang met Anny, Alice, and me at the Shangri-La for another fitting. L.A. was awake and feeling better, thanks to several hours sleep and medicinal chicken soup. Two of the items weren't yet right, so we had one more chance the next morning before my departure later that afternoon. L.A., Jonathan, and our associates were going their separate ways the next day, as well. I already missed them all.

I said goodbye to L.A. and packed all my old and new belongings, preparing to check out of the hotel. Anny and Alice arrived right on time at 9:30 a.m. and the seamstress Mrs. Chang followed with the much-improved two tops. We all said enough is enough and they are as perfect as they are going to get, and that's pretty close. I knew I would wear my clothes with pride and remember my friend every time.

I complimented Anny on the long silver-toned necklace she wore and commented on the uniqueness of the large pearls sprinkled along the chain. With a smile, she produced one of those telltale pouches I'd come to love. The type that contain jewelry. It was a duplicate necklace for me. What was I to do but once more express my appreciation for their generosity and excellent taste. We wore our twin necklaces the rest of the day.

Mr. Wu loaded my luggage, including my new purple carry-on, and we returned to the local market which I had enjoyed on my previous visit. We spent a couple of hours there as Anny and Alice answered my questions about fruits and vegetables which were strange to me. We sampled food items and perused clothing and kitchenware and had fun in the time I had left with my friends. So that I would have snacks on the train back to Taipei, Anny bought more of the nuts and dried fruit we liked. She spied one of the ingredients I needed to make her lion's head meatballs and offered to purchase some for me, but because it was dried fish and emitted an overwhelming smell, I declined. Nevertheless, she bought a small amount and I wrapped it in newspaper with hopes that the odor would be minimized, and airport personnel would not search my bags for the source.

Smiling at the usual stares and comments directed at me, I walked with Anny and Alice to the next block where the lunch crowd filled the side street. It was a magnet for people of all ages and vocations maneuvering through the area of stalls, counters, and stands to buy food. It was a timeless setting, the original version of an outdoor food court.

Two people vacated the only stools at a small counter and Anny and I quickly left the queue and claimed them, while Alice stood in line at another stall. With admiration and fascination, I watched the efficient crew serve boxed orders to the continuous flow of customers. My years as manager of our company's team initiative gave me a great appreciation of the controlled chaos happening in front of me. The kitchen must have been somewhere else, for workers constantly parked small trucks at the open rear of the space to deliver cartons of pre-boxed items to a woman who placed them in the correct location for another woman who took the money and handed boxes to the customers. It was teamwork of the highest caliber, a fluid process. I wondered how many years they had been doing that.

Anny and I ate our meal at the counter as bustling commerce transacted by hurrying people flowed around us. Just as we finished our bowls of minced meat in a thick floured gravy, and a light soup with steamed fish balls, Alice brought us wraps filled with meat and vegetables. It had taken her over twenty minutes in line to purchase them, and she was happy to take my place on the stool and join us while I stood and nibbled my wrap.

The opportunity to experience these vignettes of other cultures has made my life richer than I ever dreamed. Who else has another family in Taiwan? Who else returns to the U.S. with recipes and dried fish in their luggage? How fortunate I am.

Anny called Mr. Wu and the Winton Tile van quickly appeared to take us to a distinctly different experience. We left the sights and sounds and odors of the open market and street stalls for the refinement of an air conditioned pastry shop. The mille feuille desserts we shared were trés French and deliceux. Anny, Alice, and I sat and chatted for at least an hour, each of us aware that our time together was growing short.

We had a window of opportunity before we had to say goodbye, and Anny took me to the mattress store. On our first trip to Taiwan in 1994, L.A. and I slept so well on the hotels' exceptionally firm mattresses that we eventually ordered one for ourselves. It had been eighteen years and though it was still firm and comfortable, I had seen ads that caution consumers to replace mattresses after eight years. I thought it must be past time to purchase a new one. We made a quick stop for me to buy a replacement. Just as I was ready to purchase my selection, the salesperson told Anny, who translated for me, a surprising fact. Their mattresses are warrantied for thirty years. It seemed that I myself could wear out before that mattress did. We left the surprised woman who had just talked herself out of a sale and drove to the train station.

Anny and Alice helped me pull my large suitcase,

small carryon, and new carryon through the building. I was not allowed to buy my ticket. "This is too much, Anny," I protested. "You've done so much for me and you should not do this."

She employed her grandson Ryder's tactic and ignored me. She simply did it. The cashier paid no attention to me as they completed the transaction and Anny took the ticket, handed it to me, and said, "Jyi-fong wants to buy your ticket."

I laughed. "So, he's ready for me to leave, yes?"

Alice, Anny, and I laughed and hugged and cried. "I will miss you," I said to both those beautiful women. "I will never forget this wonderful visit."

They expressed similar sentiments to me, and with no more to say, I organized my luggage and left my friends. Perhaps we would see each other when Alice and Winston marry, but there had been no talk of planned events. Maybe Anny would come to Houston as she promised. The future was, by definition, uncertain, but of one thing I was confident. The clothes, the necklace, the shoes, the recipes, the memories, will keep my friend Anny and her family in my mind and heart forever.

The reverse trip was uneventful, as I knew what to do, how to show Alice's note to engage a taxi from the Taipei train station to the airport, how to check in and find my gate, and how to get some sleep on the long flight to Houston. After breezing through U.S. immigration and customs, I booked an Uber and dozed until the driver deposited me and my luggage at our condominium building where my familiar firm and comfortable mattress welcomed me home.

I was over jetlag by the time L.A. returned a week later, but still aglow with the memory of my trip. Every day I thought about the thanks I owed Anny and Jyi-fong, and with L.A.'s collaboration, wrote a note to them. Not an email. Not a text or WeChat message. A handwritten note on paper in an envelope addressed to their home. Or should I send it to the factory?

"Do you think Anny ever looks in their mailbox?" I asked my husband. I had never seen anyone pay attention to the box, nor had I seen mail in their home. "I know they have one. It's on the outside wall by the garage door."

"Alert someone at Winton Tile to tell Anny to look for your note," he suggested. "I agree it would be more personal if you send it to their home." I emailed to one of the staff and received instructions for sending my letter.

About a month later, I received an email from the staff person. I was aghast. "Anny and Jyi-fong liked so much hanging out with you," it read. "To thank you they are sending you a mattress. It will arrive at Swiff-Train tomorrow."

I was honored. I was embarrassed. I was so sorry that I had shopped for a mattress. I was and always will be so grateful to have such wonderful and thoughtful and generous friends. And I couldn't wait to see them again.

MARCH 2019 TAINAN

Our friends Carol and Michael Wilk invited us to join them on a 19-day cruise from Auckland, New Zealand, to Bali, and since we would be in the neighborhood, we planned to extend the trip to visit our Taiwan family. We asked the Wilks to join us, and they accepted.

Handling our combined total of twelve suitcases required the four of us to wheel the carefully stacked luggage through several airports, hotels, and garages. It was a constant challenge, but we developed a system. A better one would have been fewer clothes and thus fewer suitcases, but we thought we needed options. Our plan required each of us to roll a cart piled with our suitcases when there were carts available. Otherwise, we stacked the smaller bags on top of the larger ones and the four of us pulled our precarious loads from points A to points B, all the while cursing our need for options.

We arrived in Taipei from Bali after midnight, thus

had to stay overnight and take the bullet train to Tainan the next day. We waited outdoors in the damp heat for our airport hotel van, concerned that it would be similar to the others we had seen which were too small to accommodate our ridiculous amount of luggage. We boarded the Novotel shuttle along with eight young women, each of them traveling with only one backpack, and with relief and laughter, we all watched the driver load our bags into the spacious compartment under the bus. We were lucky and a trifle embarrassed.

It took two taxis to take us and our luggage from the hotel to the train station the next morning, and I hurried inside to find a porter or at least luggage carts. There were neither. We implemented our proven system and arrived at the correct platform with all our bags just in time to see a train depart for Tainan. We wisely had purchased tickets for the next one, knowing that our luggage process took time and we were unlikely to make that train. We had suffered no stress or anxiety and relaxed on benches to wait.

The bullet train stopped for only a very few minutes to take on passengers, and we hustled to get all our bags and ourselves on board before the doors closed. Carol and I boarded first with the smaller bags, then L.A. handled the large ones that Michael shoved from the platform into the railcar vestibule. The bags filled the aisle, the small space meant to store reasonable passengers' reasonable amount of luggage, and then the vacant seats. Meanwhile, impatient people tried to make their way around the barricade our bags created. The doors closed just as Michael had loaded the last suitcase and jumped on to the train just as the doors began to close. It took another few minutes for our exhausted guys to move our luggage into an organized cluster so that we could unload quickly when we reached Tainan.

Exhausted, we settled into our comfortable first-class seats and enjoyed naps and reading on the ninety-minute ride. The dance of unloading the luggage was a faster and easier process, and we rolled our bags and exited through the Tainan station turnstile. Smiling and handsome Jason Shu ran up to greet us. After hugs and introductions, he led us outside where Mr. Wu waited with the Winton Tile van, and we loaded into their two vehicles to drive to the Silks Place Hotel. I was happy to stay in that hotel, but disappointed that there was no door into a department store and therefore no convenient access to buy more pairs of Micanna shoes. Carol and I hoped to add a visit to the store to our itinerary. After L.A. and Michael checked us in and put our luggage in storage, Mr. Wu drove us to the restaurant where the Shens were waiting.

We hugged Jyi-fong and Anny, their son Winston, and Alice, who was now his wife. Jason had picked up his wife Betty, whom the Wilks had met when she was in Houston a couple of weeks prior to our cruise. As usual, we enjoyed a bountiful lunch as Anny, Betty, and Alice took charge of feeding Carol and me. Our men received some attention, as well, and our hosts immediately treated the Wilks with the same interest, hospitality, and attention we had always enjoyed. Already it was one bigger happy family.

Next stop was Anny and Jyi-fong's condominium. Winston and Alice had not completed the new one I visited two years prior, and still lived in their in-laws' condo, now with their five-month-old baby.

"When will you move?" I asked.

"We are too busy," Alice explained as we women rode the van to their building and Jason drove the men. "Agugu takes all my attention."

"We can't wait to meet her," I said. "Is that her Chinese name?"

She laughed as she explained that Winston started calling her that nickname and it stuck.

"What about you?" I asked Betty. "Are y'all still in this building, too?"

She answered with a smile. "You will see our new condo before you leave." She knew I wanted to.

We took off our shoes at the door and the Wilks toured the condo and learned about the elder Mr. Shen's ivory collection on display. We greeted Marina, the family housekeeper, cook, and nanny who had been with the Shens for many years and had cared for both Shen grandchildren that day while we were at lunch.

"Show them the sofa," I said to Anny. "I've never seen anything like it," I explained to the Wilks as Anny demonstrated. It is about twelve feet long but curved, with rounded ends. The back can be rolled in its track and positioned anywhere along the perimeter of the sofa that you wish. You can sit facing in any direction.

"I do this," Anny said. To keep an infant or sleeping grandchild safe, she demonstrated how to position the back around the curve of an end, making it impossible to fall off.

"It must have been fun to find that piece of furniture," I said. "It solved a problem you didn't know you had and it's a conversation piece, too."

Betty translated and Anny smiled agreement.

Carol and I took turns holding baby Agugu, who quietly stared at us and without protest allowed us to pass her around. Betty and Jason's son Ryder was now eight and seemed to warm to us sooner than he did two years ago. He kept his distance from us, though not as pointedly determined as he had been on my previous visits. He didn't hide when I smiled at him, and after a short time was brave enough to hug L.A. When prompted by Jason or Betty, he called us Agong and Ama, his third set of grandparents, but only because we're Uncle Jonathan's parents. My son is Ryder's pal, so apparently that still made us acceptable by association.

Anny honored us with a tea ceremony and served a gourmet dessert she had ordered especially for us: two cakes made of crepes spread with thin fillings, one sesame and one cream. They were delicate and delicious. The Wilks had received a gracious introduction and insight to Taiwan and our friends.

Winston drove us to the Silks Place Hotel so we could check in to our rooms and rest before Betty and Jason picked us up for the evening's agenda. We were exhausted, and they agreed that they would extend the plan and give us an additional hour to relax. We Wilks and Trains set our alarms and slept for most of the time allowed, then settled on chairs in the lobby to wait for them. Still tired, we four slid lower and lower to rest our heads on the chair backs. We waited for a full hour and wondered why Betty and Jason were so late. Because we had actually dozed in the lobby's comfortable chairs, no one had noticed the text telling us that they knew we were tired and would give us more time to rest. How thoughtful of our friends, and what a lesson we learned.

Technology has changed communication, and not always for the better. A phone call would have reached us because we would have heard the ring and answered. A text was silent and required the recipient to notice it, and no one did. The result was that we rested in public rather than in our beds, probably accompanied by a snore or snort, but those few extra winks sure felt good.

It was just the six of us, and the plan for the evening was to drive for an hour to the city of Kaohsiung to their friends' wine-tasting room and have dinner afterwards. Jason drove us in the Winton Tile van, during which time Betty and I sat closely together in the far rear seat, chatting nonstop in low voices so as not to disturb L.A. napping in the front passenger seat. I felt very grandmotherly and comfortable with her as we talked about our families and many other topics. She is as wise and perceptive as she is beautiful and intelligent.

Their friends produced rum and needed to educate the public to appreciate the spirit which is new to Taiwan. I was reminded of our early years when vinyl tile was new to our country, and the success Swiff-Train Company and Winton Tile had achieved. We tasted and discussed their products and their challenge. My favorite was the sweet dessert wine, and at $100 U.S. dollars a bottle, it certainly should have been that delicious. They served minimal snacks, and the strong rum and several additional tastings had the usual effect on me. My head was spinning. I knew standing would be a challenge, so I ended my sipping and tasting and tried not to doze while everyone else handled the alcohol better than I. By the time Betty announced it was time for dinner, I had recovered control.

Our lunch was so filling that we implored our hosts to save us from another big meal, but Betty sensibly stated that we needed food to absorb the strong rum we had consumed. Locking arms with me, she led us across the street to a casual hibachi restaurant that featured small plates. Though they were truly small, the plates kept coming. It was a light meal by Shen standards. The drive back to the hotel didn't seem as long, and after our long day, we Wilks and Trains were more than ready for sleep.

Betty was to pick up the four of us to first drive to their factory, and then to Anny's home for lunch, but the Wilks were so exhausted we excused them. At Winton Tile, L.A. and I hugged our old friends and met new staff. When he, Jason, and Jyi-fong began a serious business discussion, Betty and I left for Anny's. To my surprise, the Wilks were in the kitchen with Anny and greeted us with smiles. She had been in the hotel area and picked them up. Carol reported that even with no translator present, they had no problem communicating. I assumed that Anny had had little opportunity to practice English in the two years since our last visit, and I was proud of her accomplishment that day. Again, I chided myself for neglecting to learn more than a few Chinese words but had to confess that I was just plain lazy.

The most delicious treat was the baby. Alice and Winston arrived with Agugu, who again captivated us all. She was so good and happily allowed everyone to hold her while we sat around the kitchen table, talking and snacking. Anny always provided food.

Jyi-fong, Jason, and L.A. soon joined us, entering through a door by the kitchen that I had never noticed. "It's actually the front door," Winston told me, and I saw that there was a street where Jyi-fong had parked his car and an entrance leading into what I always thought was the rear of the house. Now I understood that the garage entry was actually at the back. Who knew?

Of course, lunch was served, prepared by Anny and Marina earlier that morning. We experienced some new dishes and some old favorites. The most unusual was a caviar that was so huge it was sliced thin on the diagonal and eaten with apple pieces and slivers of a raw white vegetable that tasted like turnip. The caviar was neither salty nor fishy, unlike the more familiar Russian delicacy. No one knew which fish produced such a large egg. Also on the menu were the lion's head meatballs and the beef noodle stew Anny had previously taught me to make. She was amused to hear that I had named that dish Anny in her honor.

I took the opportunity of the family being together and again told them that I intended to write about the friendship between the Shens and the Trains, and particularly my special connection with Anny.

Betty translated for her mother, and to me said, "Anny is happy that you are writing this. Such a friendship is rare."

L.A., Jyi-fong, Betty, and Jason retired to the living room and further business discussions while Anny, Winston, Alice, the Wilks, and I remained at the kitchen table and chatted in a relaxed mood.

"Anny," I said, "I've never asked about your family background, and how you and Jyi-fong met."

As we listened, I had the sense that her children might not have heard the story, either. Anny told it in English, careful to choose the correct words, occasionally looking to Alice or Winston for assistance and smiling at the memories.

"I worked for a man who sent me to Winton Tile and other companies for bookkeeping. I think Mr. Shen was looking for a wife for his son more than he needed a bookkeeper. He sent Jyi-fong to my company to meet me and ask me out, but I didn't accept. I had to get home after work each day. Jyi-fong kept coming and calling and asking, and I saw he was persistent, so I agreed to go out with him once."

"What did you think of him?" I asked.

"Not so good," she said, to the laughter of her audience. "Not…" She turned to Winston for translation. "Not love at first sight."

"So, what changed your mind?" I asked.

She smiled. "One day I saw him in the factory, and he was stapling wood to make pallets. I thought that he was hard working, the son of the owner and still worked hard."

"You were impressed."

"A good guy. He must not be too bad. So, I said yes I would go out with him again." She grinned. "He tried many tricks to make me happy." She thought for a moment, then added, "He still does."

"That's nice," I said. "You've been married a long time."

"It was a good decision." She paused before adding, "He has much love for his family." Further conversation confirmed that Anny believes the good far outweighs anything she would change, and she leads a rich life with friends and family. I assured her that no relationship is perfect, and we all smiled in agreement.

"I don't know anything about your own family," I said. "Tell us."

Her paternal grandparents migrated to Taiwan from Fujin province in China during the last years of the Qing Dynasty, approximately the early 1900s. They were farmers and her grandfather was also a caterer. He died before Anny was born. Her parents both lived in Tainan and had an arranged marriage. The catering business passed to Anny's parents, and her uncle inherited the farm. She was their second child among three brothers, and was 18 when her father died, 28 when she lost her mother.

"Thanks for sharing that," I said, "but another time I want to hear more."

She nodded. "Come," she said, "we will have tea."

We sat at the hinoki wood table shaped like an eagle and enjoyed Anny's tea ceremony, then Michael and L.A. rode with Jyi-fong and we girls went in Anny's car to a wood store. Not any wood store. An hinoki showroom comparable to a museum. Everything was for sale, and each item was an interesting use of the extremely hard and aromatic cypress variety native to Taiwan. All items were polished to a high butterscotch shine to enhance the grain and burl of each piece. There were tables, chairs, objets d'art, tea ceremony trays, meat cutting boards, and pigs. 2019 was the Year of the Pig, which we had learned when we saw pig sculptures in the Silks Place Hotel lobby. We were so tired at the time that I didn't question the presence of life-sized papier mâché animals in places of honor in the upscale hotel. The hinoki pigs in the showroom were anatomically correct and available with tails up, tails down, smiling, kneeling, or lying on their backs. Jyi-fong wanted Carol and me to select one item each as a gift from Anny and him, anything at all.

"I choose this," I said as I put my hand on the largest sculpture I spied, assuming it had to be one of the most expensive pieces in the showroom. We had a good laugh, and then Carol and I shopped. Of course, we were careful not to select expensive items, and considered possibilities.

"What do you think of these pigs?" Carol joked.

"Displaying those whimsical pieces in our living room would be fun, but I'll pass," I laughed. We chose small pear-shaped sculptures instead.

Our benefactor removed the stem inserts and sniffed, then rejected our first tries. "Not good," Jyi-fong said. Apparently the strength of the camphor-like aroma indicates which sculpture is made of the best wood, and he intended to give us nothing less. The chosen pears remain aromatic, and prominently reside in the Wilk and Train homes to remind us of our generous friends.

*In front of the neighborhood dumpling restaurant
Left to right: Betty, Michael, Carol, L.A., me, Anny,
Jyi-fong, Winston*

They took us to our hotel and allowed us twenty minutes to freshen up before Mr. Wu arrived to take us to our favorite dumpling restaurant. We were to meet the family for a casual dinner. The restaurant was packed, as always, but Betty had secured the one large round table for us. There was never a doubt that my seat was next to Anny, who honored me by keeping food on my plate and in my bowl. Our chairs touched each other, as did our shoulders, and occasionally I ate from Anny's plate if I saw a morsel I couldn't resist.

We introduced the Wilks to our after-meal juice bar tradition, even though no one was the least bit hungry, and the short walk to the corner helped us rationalize the additional calories we consumed.

To complete the Wilks' introduction to Taiwan, Mr. Wu drove us to the foot massage parlor. With Betty and Anny, we donned cotton shorts and sat with our feet in individual jacuzzi basins while masseurs massaged our necks, backs, and shoulders. They then escorted us to recliner chairs and worked on our feet and lower legs for forty-five minutes while we dozed, a prelude to the good night's sleep ahead.

We made plans with Betty and Anny to be ready the next morning for either shopping or the open market, and then a special lunch before our departure. Always on call, the patient Mr. Wu materialized to drive us to the hotel. Our firm, comfortable bed beckoned, and L.A. and I saved our packing for tomorrow.

Last days always arrive, and this was it. The arrangement was for Betty to pick us up at 10:30 a.m. and we would tell her whether we wanted to go to the local market or revisit the Micanna department adjacent to the Shangri La Hotel. Carol and I had been looking forward to shopping for those unique and comfortable shoes. Our husbands weren't interested in either choice, so they remained at the Silks Place Hotel.

It was Mr. Wu who came for us instead, and we drove for twenty minutes to pick up Betty. We didn't know where she had been, but she left her car in front of a building and gave the keys to Mr. Wu. He took us directly to the local open market I had visited with Anny. Carol assured me it was just like many she had seen on her travels, but she was wrong. She'd never done a market with Betty. Neither had I.

Making our way along the crowded aisles, stepping around puddles and some trash, we stopped to look over interesting kitchen utensils, then perused the produce. I asked about the unfamiliar ones. "By the way, what was the white vegetable we ate with the caviar?"

Betty showed me a large root vegetable. "It's a white carrot," she said.

I recognized it as one I had seen in Houston. "Isn't that a daikon radish?" I asked.

"Yes, I didn't think you have that in the States."

"We visited the Asian area of Houston last year," I reminded her, "don't you remember? We went to the grocery."

"Right," she said. "Do you ever use the rice cooker?"

"You mean the extra-large one you made me buy, so I can steam vegetables and eat only healthy food?"

She laughed. "You don't, do you?"

"I do, but only to cook rice." Why would Betty expect me to change at this advanced age?

"And you probably drink water with ice," she accused.

"And iced tea, and anything alcoholic." We laughed at the futile lecture Betty had given me and L.A. about the danger to one's system from drinking cold beverages. She is thin, vigorous, and beautiful because she believes in eating and drinking only the most beneficial foods in the healthiest way and wants us to do the same. "Thanks for trying, though," I said with a smile.

We companionably wandered the aisles, and stopped to sample many slivers of marinated vegetables, all delicious, and nuts with every seasoning you can imagine. Curry, cumin, pepper, cinnamon and sugar. Betty bought many varieties of nuts and vegetables to bring home for snacks before dinner. The friendly purveyors kept offering samples to us, until finally I drew the line at a pickled chicken toe. I'm sure it was special. Carol and I took that as a cue to vacate that stall area and browse a few clothing racks. I found a beautiful, embroidered peignoir set. To me it looked like a dress and long jacket which I would have worn to hostess a dinner. It expressed the inner me, but wasn't appropriate for the 76-year-old me, so it just didn't make sense to buy it. I think Carol was relieved that I had come to my senses.

After browsing the narrow aisles and navigating around the crowd of other shoppers, we left the building and met the van to return to the hotel. Our guys had checked out and stored our luggage, and we joined the Shens for our farewell lunch in a Silks Place Hotel private room.

With great ceremony, a young woman wheeled in a cart displaying a beautiful roast duck, and I knew that our hosts had again honored their visitors with an expensive and unique experience. Our friends had done so much to welcome the Wilks, and it was clear that their hospitality was sincere. How would I ever be able to reciprocate for all the wonderful times I had spent with the Shens? Would they even give me the opportunity?

Even though it was mid-day, Jyi-fong kept the toasts and wine flowing, and since we knew the train to Taipei was ideal for an afternoon nap, the Wilks and Trains toasted in return. The camaraderie, the love, the warm and gracious reception the Shens had extended to us and the Wilks had made our few days in Taiwan yet another memory for me to cherish.

Despite the mellow ambiance, the table talk changed to a practical debate about the time we should arrive at the train station for the return trip to Taipei. It was a negotiation and a test of wills. Michael and I wanted to take the 4:48 p.m. train to allow plenty of stress-free time to handle our twelve bags through both of the train stations and taxi to the Taipei airport.

"That's way too soon," L.A. said. "Our flight's not until 10:40 tonight."

Jason chimed in. "You will get to the airport four hours early"

Michael and I said in unison, "That's just fine."

Finally, L.A. seemed to acquiesce and said, "Okay, we'll leave when you say." Nevertheless, he immediately resumed the debate in an effort to convince me.

"Give it up," Winston said to him. "You're going to do what she wants." Michael and I exchanged a victorious grin.

We both hate to rush, but for different reasons. I want to do what I need to do and get it done. I think Michael stresses that he'll be late, have unforeseen challenges that he wouldn't have time to fix. I also might prefer to be in control, but that was not an important factor in our discussion, especially since I had an ally. At the end of the discussion, Michael and I thought we had prevailed and were relieved that we would have plenty of time to travel to Taipei, make the transfer to the airport, and relax before our flight.

After saying goodbye to Winston and Alice, who missed their Agugu and wanted to be home when she awoke from her nap, we left the Silks Place Hotel for Jason and Betty's new condo. The décor of dark woods and white marble floors with open spaces and contemporary fixtures was handsome, comfortable, and a perfect setting for the last moments with our friends. As if we were hungry, Betty served the snacks she had purchased the day before at the market. We enjoyed them and just hung out for two hours.

Jyi-fong and L.A. stretched out in twin recliner chairs and companionably talked and dozed, while Michael joined them between phone conversations. When I sat on the bed where Betty and Ryder were watching television in comfort, he jumped up and ran away. So much for being Grandma.

Jason and Anny took out the mahjongg set to give Carol and me my long-awaited lesson in their version of the game. We understood it but could not think nor play as fast as they. We had either won or lost before we comprehended why. The afternoon passed quickly, and I realized that we had missed the agreed upon departure time for the train station.

"Very slick, you guys," I said to L.A. and Jason.

My husband grinned as Jason said, "It was too early. But now you at last know our mahjongg."

Soon it really was time to leave for the train station and final hugs. I walked to the cars with Betty, arms and souls linked, and Carol strolled in the same manner with Anny. I was glad that our friends had enjoyed each other and had bonded. Carol and Michael expressed their appreciation to the Shens for their extraordinary hospitality, and L.A. and I did the same.

"When will you come to Houston?" I asked Anny again. "I want to see you in my home and my city."

She smiled, nodded, and said, "I will try."

With that hope, I hugged my friends one last time and took the remaining snacks Betty forced me to bring for the train. L.A. and Michael rode with Jason, Carol and I boarded Mr. Wu's van, and we went to the train station. With their assistance rolling luggage and Jason's purchase of our tickets, we proceeded to the entry turnstile. Without a ticket, our helpers couldn't accompany us farther, but Jason convinced the guards that these obviously old foreigners needed help. We did. They kept his drivers' license and allowed him to get us and our luggage on to the train, and we congratulated each other that we had made the earlier one with three minutes to spare. I told Jason that of all the nice things he'd done for me, this was the best. We would have plenty of time to process through the Taipei airport and wait for our flight. That wonderful guy almost took the trip with us, however, but jumped out the doors just as they started to close.

The three hours we spent comfortably waiting in the airport lounge gave us time to reflect on our visit with the Shens. Carol and Michael thanked us for the opportunity, and we thanked them for sharing a sample of our life. We had enjoyed each other's company and began discussing future trip possibilities.

As we walked to our gate, I experienced the same dichotomy of emotions that filled my heart and mind after each visit with Anny. Joy and gratitude for new memories to cherish, and sadness that I had no plans for my next visit with my special friend.

In truth, I would miss all the Shen family, each of them. The younger generation will occasionally come to Houston for business, and I hoped that would occur frequently and they would make time for a visit with us.

Anny and Me is a gift to my special friend, and to all my Shen family, to thank them for their gift to me: the many years of love and friendship.

But I am not sad. Our story continues. There will be so much more to write.

ACKNOWLEDGEMENTS

Without Alice Shen's gracious assistance, this book would not have become a reality. I appreciate the talents, critiques, and enthusiasm of fellow writers Warren Smith, Jean Marcoux, Pam van Scoyoc, Jean Nunnally, Karen Hale, Amanda Olson, Margo Catts, and Steve Friedman. Gratitude to my many readers for their honest feedback. And I am thankful for the encouragement and support of my friends and loved ones as I continue to write and learn.

AUTHOR

I always loved to write but had never felt compelled to do so until 1995 at the age of 52.

While working at a trade show in Hanover, Germany, I conversed with the security guard of the neighboring exhibit. We talked about life in his country after World War II, the Germany of today, and our families. This Memphis girl never expected to have such a fascinating and unique experience, and I wanted to remember every detail. Somehow I secured paper and began my first journal.

Our business took us to numerous countries and allowed us to befriend people of many cultures, and I wrote about them all. When I retired in 2018, I knew what I wanted to do with my time: write books. But what would I write about? Anything. Everything. The answers presented themselves.

My first book began as a one-page assignment for my creative writing class. *Legacy* is still a work in progress, a tale of family rivalry, domestic abuse, mystery, and love. My protagonist and her story have grown in depth and complexity along with the author who created them.

The Miracle Known as Ed Levine is fiction based on the life my friend trusted me to pen. From his birth in London during World War II to facing terminal cancer at the age of 62, his is an inspiring story of survival.

Anny and Me is a tribute to my beautiful friend and her extraordinary family. The Shens hold a special place in my heart.

If it happens, I write it. If I contemplate it, I write it. If I find a willing reader, I am honored to share my work. Through seminars, classes, and critique groups I continue to learn and make new and interesting friends. I believe that it's never too late to follow your dream. I'm doing it.

www.ingramcontent.com/pod-product-compliance
Lightning Source LLC
Chambersburg PA
CBHW071851070526
44583CB00016B/1638